Praise for *Poetry*

The simple act of an initial flick and a glance though this book immediately cemented its value for me. Within moments, I was transported, engaged, and curious; within seconds I felt resonance and familiarity. I felt understood, seen and uplifted. Within minutes I could see how this book would be of value to me over and over again.

—Tracy Sinclair, MCC
Coach, Coach Educator, Author
Past Chair, International Coaching Federation Global Board

Coaches everywhere will find ideas and inspiration in this book. The poems collected here are all written by coaches, therapists or counsellors. Each poet shares not just their poems, but their personal stories and the ideas which lie behind the poems.
The book contains helpful suggestions about how these rich materials can be used in our daily coaching practice.

Poetry for Coaching shows how we can successfully engage with and explore complex and sometimes challenging emotions and ideas by putting them into words and sharing them with others.

—Kim Morgan, MCC
Founder and Chairperson of Barefoot Coaching Ltd

This beautiful book of poetry and the stories behind them can expand the impact of your coaching. I often share a poem in my classes and personally with clients to illuminate what was learned, deepening the transformation and confidence to grow. As an adolescent, I wrote poetry to help me comprehend the world I was growing into. Reading and writing poetry opens doors to insights and reaches into recesses of our memories like music and smells of beloved foods. Savor the pages. Share them freely. I am grateful to Ross for creating this gift.

—Dr. Marcia Reynolds, MCC,
Author of *Breakthrough Coaching* and *Coach the Person, Not the Problem*

Poetry for Coaching is a beautiful collection of thoughtful and reflective poetry based around the human experiences which are often explored in coaching. The poems themselves are powerful and thought-provoking, and the sharing of the story behind each poem further enables them to touch the soul of the reader. Whilst we will all take our own personal meaning from the words, there is something special about being given a glimpse of the emotions and experiences that shaped each poem.

"An Urban Ballet" by Richard Tyler resonated with me deeply, and I'm certain that every reader will find a poem in this collection that speaks to them.

This collection beautifully demonstrates how poetry can serve as a catalyst for personal growth and transformation, both in coaching and in life.

—Ruth Randall PCC
MD at Animas Centre for Coaching

Sometimes feeling deeply heard and seen and felt by another in a conversation is enough to bring new insight. At other times, the line or the rhythm of a story or a poem can offer a little bit more. Something that sits with a person, holds them or gently offers a phrase that unlocks something. Which makes this book a great resource for anyone who has conversations with other people.'

—Claire Pedrick MCC
Founder, 3D Coaching
Author – *The Human Behind the Coach, Simplifying Coaching*

Poetry for Coaching - Transformation Through Verse, edited by Ross Nichols, offers a unique and deeply reflective collection of poems written by coaches, therapists, and counsellors. The anthology explores universal themes including connection, love, acceptance, forgiveness, resilience, and the journey of life itself. Each poem serves as a gateway into the emotional and psychological experiences that define our human existence.

What makes this book particularly powerful is the personal depth each contributor brings, blending their professional expertise with raw, authentic expression. As a result, the verses are not just literary, but also therapeutic—inviting readers to engage in introspection, healing, and personal growth. The poems resonate with a sense of empathy, guiding readers through the complexities of transformation with wisdom and grace.

This collection is both a gentle companion for those on a personal development journey and an insightful resource for professionals in coaching and therapy. Through the power of verse, *Poetry for Coaching* illuminates pathways to resilience and emotional freedom, making it a valuable addition to any bookshelf, especially to those in coaching, mentoring and therapeutic professions.

> —Jayne Morris MCC, ICF UK Associate Board Member
> Coach, Trainer & Supervisor
> Author: *Burnout to Brilliance*

Coaches have straightforward ways of how to coach galore: competency methods, models and techniques. Those have their strengths and need mastering first. No doubt. Then, we have recent AI approaches to coaching: the algorithms of matching and asking questions, the chat-bots of goal attainment, to name just two.

And then we have *Poetry for Coaching* as a sideways approach for how to coach clients to understand and appreciate themselves and the world around them, especially one that is full of portrayals of the ugly, chaotic, violent and merciless ways of being and going about life.

Poetry for Coaching is of great value as a bridge in that world. Its strength lies in how to artfully bare open human vulnerabilities with depth and empathy. As clients embrace the power of empathy through poetry, they have access to how to come together again, helping them understand themselves and one another with connection, love, acceptance, forgiveness and resilience.

This book is ideal for clients who appreciate having truth sneaking up on them. It is for clients who appreciate 'understanding' through how deep meaning can be felt in details.

Poetry for Coaching is the aesthetic choice of coaches to explore with clients what is beautiful in and through life for them. It is ideal for coaches who seek to support clients in expressing their emotions and connecting to those emotions. As such, it helps clients improve their literacy in thriving, and it helps coaches improve their literacy in coaching.

> —Dr Tunde Erdos MCC
> Executive Coach and Supervisor

I found this anthology deeply inspiring and rich with insights, making it a powerful resource in my coaching practice. Each poem offers a unique lens for reflection, allowing me to explore deeper emotions and thoughts with my clients. I see endless opportunities to use the poems as prompts for introspection and personal growth, helping individuals process events and challenges in their lives. Whether for personal use or to guide meaningful conversations, these poems and accompanying stories are invaluable for fostering self-awareness and encouraging exploration in a way that feels both gentle and profound. A must-have for any coach seeking creative tools.

—Sarah Manley
Introvert Career Coach, Mentor and Author of *The Quiet Catalyst*

Poetry and stories are some of the oldest, most profound pathways we have into something greater; the currents of connection, transformation, and the love and heartbreak of existing. They invite us to sit with them, to walk with them, to see others in their fragile, powerful humanity, and so to remember our own. This book gives you a simple, precious invitation to meet yourself and others in all the myriad struggles and gifts of living. By putting brief, honest, stories alongside poetry born from them, the book creates so many different ways to take a breath, and shift perspective on what you are going through, or simply drop into it. It brings poems to open up the heart and mind, and to connect to something within and without, freeing you up to meet life more fully, as you are.

—Dave Rock
Poet, storyteller, creator of Flow Speaking
www.flowspeaking.com

There's a lot of talk among coaches about transformative experiences – perhaps because change is at the heart of what we aspire to for our clients, our communities, and often for ourselves. But the term tends to be over-used. So when I was invited to read a book about the transformative power of poetry, I approached it with some trepidation.

What a surprise, therefore, to discover that this collection delivers what it promises. Each poem, and each of the accompanying stories penned by coaches, counsellors and therapists, draw the reader into conversations, sparking curiosity and opening up new perspectives.

Whether you're already an aficionado of poetry or relatively unfamiliar with this literary genre, this book may change the way you read and reflect. Engage with it in any way you choose – either select a poem on a topic that resonates with you here and now, or open the pages at random and see where it takes you.

It might spur you to action or invite you to pause, it might dare you to reach a decision or urge you to reconsider. It's not only the range and depth of the musings - on topics as far-ranging as love, connection, acceptance, forgiveness, resilience - that will intrigue and inspire. It's also the vulnerability and authenticity of the writers that may change how you feel, how you think, what you do and ultimately, who you are.

—Juliet Landau-Pope PCC
JLP Coach, productivity coach for students and young adults
www.jlpcoach.com

I've read poetry all my life and used it in my coaching for many years. Like other art forms poetry goes beyond the logical and visible, has a short cut to the emotions and so allows us to connect with or interpret our clients in subtle and transformative ways. Tracy Sinclair's foreword to this book explores this eloquently and I am glad to have read the book for that alone.

Strangely, thereafter I found the stories of how the poems were written more beguiling than the poems themselves. It is touching that the writers have opened themselves and their emotions in 2 ways. With its bouncing rhythms, The Dare by Sarah Moores speaks to the many new and scary possibilities our work as coach offers us ...if we dare. These coaches (and therapists) have dared to share!

—Jenny Bird MCC
Director JB Executive Coaching Ltd, Executive Coach, Coaching Supervisor

Brilliance, Genius, Heartfelt, Transformational and so much more, *Poetry For Coaching* feels like Poetry for the soul.

A journey that takes you for a breath-taking ride through creating Connection, Love, Acceptance, Forgiveness, Resilience & Life and just when you think you're done, you take one final journey.

The journey back home to who you really are.

Each line, snippet and poem speaks to you and wakes you up that little bit more to unlock the riches and treasures within you and your life right now.

What each poet has written isn't just words, art or poetry, but a story about you if you read close enough.

Prepare to be impacted and served so deeply.

—Raghav Parkash
Executive Life Coach & Personal Confidant to High Performing Leaders
www.raghavparkash.com

I am impressed by this book! It touches a coach's soul at a deep level. I've recognized myself in so many of the poems and can see how I can use these in my own coaching. The book is laid out in a way that enables the reader to open to a section appropriate to their current circumstance to find the exact poem they need at that moment. The stories behind each poem offer a deeper richness that underlies the poem itself. Thank you for providing such a delightful and greatly needed resource to the coaching profession!

—Kathy Harman MCC, CRC
Coach, Director of Education at Radiance Partners LLC

'As a coach & supervisor, I have used poetry for years. Poetry taps into a part of us that is often hard to describe or even connect to. Poetry touches people, it evokes a feeling, a sense of something that's often intangible. This book of treasured poems connects us all, both the poems and the personal stories. I particularly love the way the poems are grouped by human experience.

I am looking forward to using this book at future retreats and with clients. Thanks for bringing it out into the world'.

—Claire Palmer MCC
Coach & Supervisor, Author of *A Little Witch in Waiting*

In my 30+ years of coaching, I have always loved that liminal space; that transition period from just before a coaching begins with the undiscovered landscapes and narratives of a client, to those moments where soul is revealed, where the client's own truth appears and where rivers of emotion are free to be witnessed – new perspectives becoming available.

Poetry is its own form of coaching – offering that liminal space at any moment to anyone who is willing to step into that space of external and ethereal verse to internal moments of surprise, delight and awakening.

This collection is a juicy reminder of how we as coaches can be touched by a juxtaposition of words or breath; the flutter of the client's eye or the inflection that reveals all.

I am using this as a little incantation to myself – opening up the collection randomly and letting it inspire me to become just that much more present to the client, myself and the infinite and intimate space between us.

Here's what grabbed me from Encrypted Love by Basia Henderson:

> *But know that one day*
> *Another messenger will be knocking on your door,*
> *And another...*
> *And another...*
> *Until you receive the message with grace*

Enjoy.

—Libby Robinson, MCC
Managing Partner – Integral
www.integralcoaches.com
Director of Coach Training, Advanced Coaching Practicum

The idea of poetry and the narrative behind them is always mesmerizing. The connection between counselling, mindful conversations, and everything in between, whether spoken or unspoken, is important to be noticed. Poetry is a means to heal ourselves, our trauma, our scars and helps us to grow as humans. Therefore, this book is significant to read as it strengthens our power as poets, educators, therapists, and overall, as human beings.

—Kadek Sonia Piscayanti
Poet, founder of the Singaraja Literary Festival, author of *Mindful & Creative Learning of EFL Poetry* & the *Burning Hair* poem anthology.

POETRY for COACHiNG

Transformation Through Verse

by **The Creative Coaching Collective**

Edited by **Ross Nichols**

Cover image by: LongMoose Graphics
Book design by: SWATT Books Ltd

Printed in the United Kingdom
First Printing, 2024

ISBN: 978-1-0685148-0-7 (Paperback)
ISBN: 978-1-0685148-1-4 (eBook)

The Creative Coaching Collective
Salisbury, Wilts, SP1 3NH

info@transitiontransformers.co.uk

To everyone whose life has been enriched through poetry.

"Poetry is an echo, asking a shadow to dance."

CARL SANDBURG

Contents

Foreword 1

The simple act of an initial flick and a glance though this book immediately cemented its value for me. Within moments, I was transported, engaged, and curious; within seconds I felt resonance and familiarity. I felt understood, seen and uplifted. Within minutes I could see how this book would be of value to me over and over again.

One of the many great teachers from whom I have had the privilege of learning, Michael Grinder, created a model of human development which never ceases to inspire me. I have experienced many situations where this model has guided me and helped me to understand where I am and what I need to do next and is one that I love to share with others, especially for our development as Coaches. *Poetry for Coaching* is a perfect example of this model in action.

Grinder's model is called The Science and The Art. The more commonly used term is: 'The Art and Science of...*something*", however Michael challenges the order of this wording and proposes that it is the Science that comes first. When we first learn to coach (or indeed, when we first learn to do anything), it is important to focus on essential skills, the tools and techniques, and be able to consistently apply and work with the competencies associated with that activity. In the case of coaching, we have several models of coaching competence available to us, as well as the foundations of coaching psychology and adult development theories – all of which underpin the 'science' of our work as practitioners.

However, coaching is also defined as a 'creative process' and this creativity applies just as much to the coach as it does to their client. Creativity in coaching includes thinking or feeling differently about things, considering things from a different perspective and inviting ourselves to go beyond our habitual patterns of processing, responding and deciding etc. Words and language offer a rich palette of literal colour; a creative channel, which invites the speaker and the listener to access a new domain of exploration and possibility. This is creativity; this is art in motion as a conversation unfolds.

As we gain consistent proficiency with the science, the art and the artist within us can emerge. Through imagery, metaphor, symbolism and the paralleled contexts that poetry can yield between what is real and what could be real, if only we were to let our creative wisdom have voice, we can find ourselves evolving and growing in ways we might not have imagined. The subtitle of this book is so apt: *Transformation through Verse...* as the words and their meaning literally transform us to new ways of conceptualisation and levels of experience.

Poetry for Coaching however, goes beyond poetry. It offers the story behind each poem, which beautifully mirrors how we, as practitioners, invite our clients to share more about the meaning and stories behind their own words. Poetry, whether it is engaged with by the writer/speaker or the reader/listener, is highly evocative, and allows for deeper understanding, connection, resonance and empathy, as well as nurturing the trust and safety of the practitioner-client relationship.

Both the poems and the stories behind them invite us into a deep, inner space within the Poet. Sometimes that space is full of awe and wonder; sometimes it is full of pain and loss and a myriad of other human emotions accessible to us all, if we allow them. The wonderful coaches, counsellors and therapists who have contributed to this book have opened their hearts to us, bared some of their soul to us and shown us their truth, their vulnerability and their whole self in a simple, clean and transparent way. We can only invite our clients to go as far as we are prepared to go ourselves, and this collective work is a powerful, creative and inspiring invitation and permission to others to do the same.

Since that first glance, I have picked up the book many times already, discovering new poems and revisiting others; inevitably finding something that connects with me. This book is a gem of a resource to keep close to hand, for that simple flick of the page and glance at the words will evoke something useful and creative for our own process, as well as that of our clients.

Tracy Sinclair, MCC
Coach, Coach Educator, Author
Past Chair, International Coaching Federation Global Board

Foreword 2

As a coach and a coach trainer, I have always been an avid collector of poems and literary quotes, sharing them with my coaching and supervision clients and incorporating them into my business' learning materials and teaching practice.

When I started my company many years ago, I took its name – Barefoot – from a line in a poem. The words of this poem are in big letters on the walls of our offices today.

A particular feature of the poems in this collection is that all the poems are written by coaches, therapists and counsellors. The writers share their poems and also the stories behind their writing, their personal struggles with life's challenges and their triumphs.

Poems engage our hearts and minds. They speak to our experiences, our fears and our hopes. Poems and stories can make learning experiences memorable and help us to see more clearly and better understand our own life and the lives of others.

Finding, reading and sharing poems can be a safe and exciting way to explore complex and challenging issues and feelings. So can writing poems!

I am looking forward to using poems and stories from this collection in my own coaching work. I hope that many readers will, like me, find insight, joy and inspiration within the pages of this book.

Kim Morgan, MCC
Founder and Chairperson of Barefoot Coaching Ltd

Foreword 3

This collection of poetry is a profound expression of the internal world of each author.

Triggered by life events – loss, separation, fear and emotional rollercoasters – the writers elegantly express their own feelings and vulnerabilities.

They encourage you the Reader to stop, be still, be present, and notice moment to moment the richness and fullness of the world around you.

Only in present moment awareness is found the love, connectedness and abiding fulfilment that we all seek.

This is your invitation to turn inwards, to take your lampshade off, challenge your self-imposed rules or limitations, listen to the infinite knowledge and wisdom you have always possessed, and start living life as the freedom and joy that is your true essence.

Brandon Bays
Founder of The Journey Method and International Best-Selling Author of *The Journey*, *Freedom Is*, *Living the Journey*, and *Light in the Heart of Darkness*

Note from the Editor

THE IDEA FOR THIS BOOK came from the simple observation that insightful poems, coupled with the stories behind them, were being shared informally on social media by other coaches. I began wondering aloud whether this represented an untapped resource that could contribute to our collective wellbeing. A peer coach, Hazel Martin, heard my pondering and, as a good coach would, asked me what was stopping me from bringing this idea to life. My answer took me by surprise: nothing was stopping me! In that moment, I gave myself permission to launch this project, which has been a joy to work on ever since. I am grateful to all the coach poets who submitted poems for consideration – this Anthology would not exist without your poems and stories. It has been shaped by a group of coaches with a passion for poetry, who became the Creative Coaching Collective, and my co-editors: Anjli Gheewala, Kate Jenkinson, Tracey McEachran, Sarah Moores, Elizabeth Papalia and Sharon Strimling. My sincere thanks to them all for their collaboration and support in collecting and selecting these poems and stories with me and so much more besides. My thanks go to Elizabeth Papalia for her support with my use of English. A special mention goes to Sharon Strimling for editing all the poems and stories with great care and sensitivity to our poets' art; and to Sarah Moores for her guidance and support with curating this Anthology to enhance the Reader's experience. I'm grateful to Lisa Longmoose, who designed the cover and, with infinite patience and flexibility, formatted our manuscript into a viable publication; and to our publishing facilitator, Samantha Pearce at SWATT Books Ltd, whose guidance and support was invaluable. Thanks are due to Gill Frost, who helped me with initial project planning and technical support, and to Anjli Gheewala who stepped up to become assistant project manager.

Our commitment is to distribute fifty percent of the profits from the sale of this Anthology to philanthropic causes.

About This Book

POETRY FOR COACHING IS an anthology of poems and the stories behind them, written by coaches, counsellors, and therapists to support personal transformation, empowerment and healing. This book provides a unique opportunity for the reader to benefit from the depth of experience of qualified coaches and therapists who have faced and overcome rich and textured life challenges. Here they share with you their insights and learning — through the power and beauty of poetry and prose.

We can all feel stuck at times, limited by difficult experiences. It's not always clear where to find support. Here, as we read the words of others, we can find comfort, insight, and even challenge. Here, in other's poems and stories, we can find ourselves, and then move beyond our current understanding to new perspectives and new possibilities.

Poetry, in its brevity and elegance, engages us with layered meanings. It can take us beyond the words on the page to touch our very souls. As Phillip Pullman, author of *His Dark Materials*, wrote:

"Poetry is not a fancy way of giving you information; it's an incantation. It is actually a magic spell. It changes things; it changes you."

From early in my coaching career, I found myself spontaneously sharing poems and stories with my clients. When I did, they almost always found them useful. Later I began to write my own poems and sometimes shared these with my clients, which were generally well received. What I've noticed is that poetry and storytelling can help people to:

- Connect to others' experience.
- Gain insights into their own experience.
- Be present to their own emotions and go deeper into themselves.
- Reframe their experience.
- Gain fresh perspectives.
- Provoke new ways of thinking about themselves and their situation.
- Evoke awareness of their uniqueness.
- Equip themselves emotionally and spiritually for the current stage of their life journey.
- Realise they are not alone, that others have walked the same path.
- Poetry can also be used as part of a coach's reflective practice.

Storytelling adds richness and context to the poems. Combining stories with poems heightens the impact of both: one can unlock new meaning in the other. Applying poetry and storytelling to coaching enhances the art of coaching by enlarging the coaching space, enabling new possibilities to emerge.

How to Use this Book

THE READER MAY WISH to read the stories first, then the poems or vice versa – both approaches are equally valid. The Anthology has been curated into chapters based on themes that are the stuff of coaching: Connection; Love; Acceptance; Forgiveness; Resilience; Life. These themes may be used to guide the reader when seeking support for a specific challenge.

The book can also be read more generally for inspiration and for the sheer beauty of the poems and stories. If you've never read a poem before, you are in the right place! Simply relax, suspend judgement, and let your curiosity draw you to whatever it is you need in this moment, be that a poem or a story. Or perhaps you are a coach, counsellor or therapist and see the value in using this resource in your practice. Whatever your approach, I hope this Anthology brings you joy as well as inspiring transformation, empowerment and healing for yourself or those with whom you work.

The poems and stories in this Anthology cover a wide range of human experience. Readers who are adversely affected by any of the content should seek appropriate professional support.

CHAPTER 1

CONNECTION

"So often, when we feel lost, adrift in our lives, our first instinct is to look out into the distance to find the nearest shore. But that shore, that solid ground, is within us. The anchor we are searching for is connection, and it is eternal."

BRENÉ BROWN

The state of being in "connection" is something that most people hold onto closely in their lives. Research indicates that having meaningful connections can enrich one's life and provide meaning beyond the mundane rhythm of existing. Most connections come and go, which sets us up for moments of heartache, disappointment or perhaps relief and joy – what comes is a poetic exploration of this theme. (Research gathered by the Centre for Wellbeing and presented by the New Economics Foundation in 2008).

Elizabeth Papalia

Story behind
You're Not That Far...
by Humaira Naz

I WROTE THIS POEM during the 2020 lockdown. Not having anticipated the lockdowns, and living far from family and friends, I wrote this poem for all of us who felt a loss of connection. For me, lockdown was a drastically changing time, and all the so-called little things we can miss in the best of times, became even more tender, such as the twinkle in a loved one's eye. This poem is an expression of love and loss, and the deeper appreciation that can come with that loss, even if it is temporary.

You're Not That Far...
by Humaira Naz

You're not that far,
Yet I have to wait till I can see you again.

You're not that far,
Yet I can't reach out and hold you.

You're not that far,
Yet your presence for now remains a memory.

You're not that far,
Yet the waiting seems to get longer, even when it is not.

You're not that far,
Yet watching your lips move as you speak,

And rise as you smile,
Brings your presence here to me.

You're not that far,
Yet that twinkle in your eye is clearer the closer we are.

You're not that far, yet
I MISS YOU.

Story behind
Just For One Minute
by Tracey McEachran

I WROTE THIS POEM IN 2021, towards the end of the first lock down. I was so busy online, coaching individuals and teams, that I barely had time to rest. The same was true for those I coached.

I work predominantly with clients in the social housing sector, a sector profoundly challenged in the early days of covid. The organizations I worked with had very little infrastructure to enable their workers to work from home, and they also employed front line workers. Many of my clients were working with vulnerable families and individuals, as well as running care homes and hostels.

At one point, between calls, I managed to grab a moment for myself. I sat with my face to the sun. Later I wrote this poem.

Throughout the pandemic, I read *Just For One Minute* frequently to the groups I coached. It helped them to stop and take in the fullness of their lives. It helped them to take a breath before we started our sessions.

Just For One Minute
by Tracey McEachran

Just for one minute
I sat in the sun
Just for one minute
bathed in light
in warmth
Just for one minute
I felt the presence of you
just as the sky turned
grey to blue
Just for one minute
I let myself rest
breathed deeply
filling my chest
Just for one minute
I let my mind drift
Just for one minute
allowed the stress to drain
Just for one minute
in one whole day

Story behind
Connection, Recollection, Time
by Tracey McEachran

I CREATE IMAGES WITH PHOTOGRAPHY. My imagery often works with psychological and emotional themes. I find these difficult to write about in prose, as I am reluctant to pin down any meaning for the viewer. With poetry, I find I can put my images to words in a way that leaves room for interpretation and one's own meaning.

I live on the South coast of England. At the time I wrote this poem, I was out every day walking my dog through fields by the shore. It was a new routine, and I loved it and was present to the walks. A routine is grounding and wonderful, but can also make time pass all too quickly if we sleepwalk through it.

Time fascinates me. I see it with my art, where every image is a sort of death. In a split second an image is captured – never to come again. I work with analogue film, which holds more romance for me than digital.

Images, like time, have become disposable. Where we once took one or two images, we now snap hundreds, and discard as many. We seek perfection, and in so doing miss so much beauty. We view life through screens, go for a meal and snap every course. Who would have done that with a film camera, I wonder.

When someone asks you about a memory, instead of scrolling through your phone to find a picture, can you bring it to life in the creative corners of your own mind?

Connection, Recollection, Time
by Tracey McEachran

Time falls through your fingers
when you lift your hand from the sand
Each minute so small you may not notice when they fall

Stand still for a while. Look around
Absorb the treasure that you are
Notice each glimmer of every star
calling for your attention
Look away from your gadgetry, distracting from your intention
to be, to write, to see
Breathe life, hour by hour, minute by minute

Stand still, live free
Understand who you want to be
What fears hidden deep inside keep you running, never becoming
the watcher, the waiter, the meditator
Absorb each second
Catch each glint
Feel each grain fall through your hand

Can you see the kiss of sunlight, illuminating each fragment
Do you witness each moment of wonder
Or are you like me
blind to each miniature blade of grass that goes unnoticed
like the minute that has passed
You transition through this land
like little grains of sand falling through your hands

Story behind
Soul
by Tracey McEachran

IN LATE SPRING OF 2022, I embarked on a wilderness vigil. The vigil ran for seven days and seven nights. Four nights were solitary, with only a sleeping bag, a tarp, a bivy bag and water. As I mentally prepared for the vigil, two poems surfaced. Faced with being stripped of everything but bare existence, my unconscious had served up these two poems of soul and spirit.

Seven days deep in nature without a phone; four nights with just my thoughts and the spirits of the woods. I am still processing the magic of these experiences.

As a coach, I see myself as a soul and spirit worker. I am often asked how I can see into another's soul. The truth is I can't. I just listen and soul speaks.

Soul
by Tracey McEachran

Soul is of the earth
of all things bound to our humanness
It lives in the shadow, the deepness of us
a sadness that knows we must die
Through death all we love will be taken

There is a sweetness and a yearning
that comes from our soul
the need to belong
to be seen and heard
to know our existence is not in vain

When we walk in the woods
we feel our soul
sink our hands into soil
Our soul knows that is our destiny
to become good soil, make way for new life

We speak of soulmates
the one who can journey with us
diminish the sorrow of aloneness
take away the bittersweet pain of existence
It is our soul that weeps, loves deeply
It cannot be denied
Our soul will not be put aside

We witness the products of our soul's disconnection
rampant consumerism, hate, intolerance
We, half-alive, numb, avoid seeing ourselves
seeing the pain of us
It is within the soul where our fears lie

But when we see our fear, we bring kindness
Our spirits soar from our mortal confines
the yin and the yang of us
one cannot be without the other

This is the work of the soul
to ground us, embrace our body's limitations
our aloneness

Feed your soul
Free your spirit

Story behind
Spirit
by Tracey McEachran

IN LATE SPRING OF 2022, I embarked on a wilderness vigil. The vigil ran for seven days and seven nights. Four nights were solitary, with only a sleeping bag, a tarp, a bivy bag and water. As I mentally prepared for the vigil, two poems surfaced. Faced with being stripped of everything but bare existence, my unconscious had served up these two poems of soul and spirit.

Seven days deep in nature without a phone; four nights with just my thoughts and the spirits of the woods. I am still processing the magic of these experiences.

As a coach, I see myself as a soul and spirit worker. I am often asked how I can see into another's soul. The truth is I can't. I just listen and soul speaks.

Spirit
by Tracey McEachran

And the spirit said
Fly
As high as you can
Soar above the earth
Wander to the four corners
Of existence

Look down to see
The earthiness of the soul
Know it is kept safe in good soil
Holding on to the earth
An act that allows you to fly free
Tethered so you may wander far
Far from the tree where you were conceived

Fly
Over the mountains
Across the oceans
The vastness that is yours
Let the wind take your wings
Trust you will fly where you need

The key to possibility is trust
You are free to soar beyond the confines
Of your soul
Fly above the clouds in the light
Where sunlight, moonlight
Cast no shadow

Know it is your destiny to see the future
The possibilities of everything
No limitations, no restrictions
Twins held in the soul

Fly
Beyond yourself, your borders
To a place of total freedom
Of endless hope
Unbound creativity

Through your third eye
Leave the constraints of earth
To a timeless immersion
Where a second feels like an hour
An hour passes by in a second

And the spirit says
Close your eyes
And fly

Story behind
Together
by Gillian Walter

THIS IS A LONG and gentle, yet profound story of my journey back to my inner child and true self. After half a century of holding poems and art inside – conditioned to believe that they, and any form of creativity, were lazy and worthless – I somehow landed in a creativity course for supervisors. As I signed up, I think I had some form of art therapy application in mind, and perhaps bringing creativity to client sessions seemed 'serious' enough to justify its exploration.

The outcome was more valuable to both me and my clients than I could have imagined. I came out of years of hiding my work as weird, different, or even wrong. I reconnected with who I am at my core: fascinated, compassionate and curious about people. I found a safe space, not only to create, but to acknowledge and value who I am, how I think, and the way I work as a coaching supervisor.

This connection back to my unique self was an intense experience in and of itself, but the effect did not end there. I found myself connecting on a much more natural and deeper level, not only with clients, but with family and friends too. In connecting back to myself, connecting with everyone became deeper, quicker, and easier.

Together
by Gillian Walter

On my journey from there to here,
I met someone without a fear -
No care or worry held them back,
And giggling at my weighty pack,
They skipped and danced along the road,
Curious of my tired load.
They quizzed me when, how and why
I chose to march instead of fly?
Why my wings were cased in lead,
When I could dance with them instead?

On my journey from there to here,
Their 'giggle-skip' joy warmed my ear.
My feet and wings recalled the beat,
Dancing together in the street.
Perhaps I was too outrageous,
But true heart beats being contagious,
I lost track of how high we flew,
But, oh my goodness, what a view -
Creative hearts in connection,
Mirrored in every direction!

On my journey from here to there,
Around again and everywhere,
My giggle and I walk as one -
We dance, we sing and have such fun,
Inviting others to the song,
Voices ripple high and strong.
Creating melodies brand new,
As old as time in me and you.
Nature's rhythm keeps on ringing
To Choirs of Brave Voices singing.

Story behind
Embrace
by Julia Heubeck

THIS POEM DESCRIBES AN embrace I experienced that was unlike any other I had previously felt. This embrace was a key, and it unlocked a door to the purest of connections with another human being. This connection was unique, as for the first time I felt free from all my past experiences with masculine energy. I was allowed to fully inhabit my feminine self, and felt accepted in a way I had never before experienced. My body and my soul remember that moment to this day. And though it was so powerful, I don't need to experience it again. That time was enough.

Embrace
by Julia Heubeck

Where infinity meets, we meet too.

We came here through the simplest of agreements,
A contract signed outside of time and space.

This is not fate or will,
We anchor in a different place.

In stillness we surrender to fusion,
A touch beyond flesh and grasp.

We have no need to meet again,
This union has no future and no past.

And still, I cannot help
but feel a sense of wonder,
about the wisdom our meeting brings.

The Yin takes on another meaning,
A Yang once unbeknownst to Men.

It is your darkness which ignites my shining,
Polarity has never felt so whole.

The quiver I now feel inside,
A burning whisper of your soul.
The quiver turns into a ripple.

I sense the currents of a wave.
We are the movement of the ocean,
Entangled in divine embrace.

Story behind
Alone Together
by Richard Tyler

I LOVE JUXTAPOSITION. PARADOX. I like holding both/and, not simply either/or. My last 12 months has been a swell of ugliness and beauty. I have been caught in a liminal space; passing from here to there. Landing somewhere between no longer and not yet...

Within all of that, I am mystified as to how two seemingly opposing qualities, sit side by side. To begin with, I found it destabilising. In time, it was like having 2 friends who, despite the differences, got on well and held mutual ground.

It's always worth including the opposite. What is it for you? What role does it bring? How might it serve you to practise holding both? You see, when you do, the battle is dismantled. We take apart the inner wrestling. It can gently settle. You can gently settle.

Alone Together
by Richard Tyler

The neatness and the beauty
The disorder and the ugliness
The ease and the flow
The difficulty and the struggle
So much love
So much brutality
The lightness and the joy
The heaviness and the despair
Everyone close
No one to be seen
The clarity
The confusion
Pure silence
Relentless cacophony
Holding it all firm
Holding nothing
Such simplicity
Such complexity
The fullness
Now empty
No longer
Not yet
Me
You
Not here
Not there
Alone
Together

Story behind
The Circle
by Anna Springett

IN 2020, I WAS DUE to start a diploma with a group of colleagues from all over the world; we were to meet for in-person training in London over a series of modules that year. Then, of course, the pandemic hit and everything went online.

On day two of the programme, I was awaiting covid test results to find out if I could go to hospital for some rather intimidating tests: Alongside lockdown and all the shared anxieties of 2020, my family and I experienced a number of significant health scares. I received the 'all okay' news from one family member, only to get caught in another round of worrying doctors' visits for another. Right after this second 'all clear', and at the start of what should have been the exciting beginning to a long-awaited global programme, I began a scary journey of my own.

What should have been a two-week turnaround became a torturous month of delays due to the impact of coronavirus. It all ended well, thank goodness, but until I knew the outcome, I had to live with the worst sort of 'not knowing'.

In the midst of all of this, I was determined not to let what was going on in my personal life impact on how I experienced the beginning of the diploma. As I wrote to my fellow learners the following day, 'I had been so looking forward to the module, to the joy of connecting and learning together, that I wanted to leave all of this aside for the two days. Inevitably, and especially on Day 2, I struggled, and was quite distracted. Thank you for allowing my process, whether you knew it or not, and for holding a space for each of us to be, however brave, and however much of ourselves came to the fore.'

This poem captures my experience of arriving into a group of new others, holding hope for the human connections and relational possibilities that resided there, alongside all of what life was throwing at me at that time: 'If I have all of this going on in my life, each and every other person around this circle will have their own stories to tell, whether of pain, sorrow or happiness.' I chose to stay open and hopeful.

The Circle
by Anna Springett

Here I come
Weighed down and light-footed
Here I come
Stressed and broken
Warm and hopeful
Here I come.

I come with all that is scared
and lonely, worn and raw
I come with my joy and dreams
and cherished memories
My energy, ideas... *and my heart*.
My relationships
My history
My greatest achievements and deepest passions

With every wound and mark that life has rendered me –
I come.
And I sit in this circle,
A smiling, warm and human face
Extending love and cautious vulnerability
To the cavernous, exquisite others
That I meet here.

Story behind
An Urban Ballet
by Richard Tyler

AS A CHILD, I would watch my Dad take to his bench. It was the sanctuary that he retreated to when he needed to step off his frantic wheel of life. In my adult years, I yearned for a bench in our garden. I wanted my own place to dwell; a pause, a space between the notes, somewhere I could rest in those moments in between. Well, I found one. I sanded it down with tenderness and great love. I painted on protector that would do its work to keep the wood safe, healthy and continuing to live on with me as its new guardian.

It became *my* sanctuary. The more I sat, the more I observed. I paid attention to the nature around me and my own true nature that rested somewhere deep inside.

I see benches as so much more than just somewhere to perch. They are our own public places of storytelling. I hope my insights about the view from a bench encourages you to pay greater attention when you next pass one. What has it seen? What tales have played out there? How have lives been stirred by their interaction with that bench? And perhaps reflect on your own place to dwell; do you have one? Do you need one? When the wheel of your own life feels a little too much, what holds you and soothes you in the way that my bench holds me?

An Urban Ballet
by Richard Tyler

A place that bears witness to an entire lifecycle; each flash of the 24/7 Urban Ballet is visible from here

It is, by far, the best seat in the house

It falls somewhere on our journey as we leave home

The red breasted robin who settles on the backrest as he goes about his morning routine, stopping to survey his kingdom

The pregnant mum who perches to rest, through to the long married couple who reminisce about life...to the plaque that honours their presence

Babies are conceived here

Life is taken away here

It sees everything

The secrets that are never shared

It holds every tale, never revealing the truth

The scene of merry hello's and heart breaking goodbye's

New mums unite and share their anecdotes of both the joy and the despair of parenthood

The toddlers first tantrum

Teenage gangs who have it as their mission control

The first meeting

The first kiss

The last kiss

The broken heart

The mourning of loss

Truths revealed

Lies concocted

A place to be private, in public

A spot for solitude

A social gathering

The empty bag of Frazzles that is tightly folded and tucked amongst the slats

The place to create

Plans are hatched

Ideas are born

'Dean woz ere 96', inscribed with his makeshift knife, adorns the armrest.
'Fuck U Dean' is etched in just beneath
Memories are made
A theatre where free performances run round the clock
Judgements are passed
The world is put to rights
Laughter rings out
Canoodling couples
Giggling girls
Lost travellers
New insights and perspectives gained.
The pause between places – the moment of rest within a liminal space
A space between the notes
Where we stop to offload the burdens of life
Where we can survey; the world outside and the world inside
A place to dwell
A bijou space in the melee of the metropolis where it is acceptable to do nothing,
to consume nothing, to just be
The modest bench doesn't turn anyone away
It is someone's home
Somewhere we can catch our breath
Somewhere where the final breath is taken
The bench will contain whatever it is offered
It is both the auditorium and the stage of life
It holds every guest with the same firmness. Supportive. Unconditional
The place we pass as we journey home
Life, death, and everything in between...
The humble bench, sees it all.

Story behind
Finders' Keepers
by Elizabeth Papalia

AS AN IMAGINATIVE, CREATIVE HUMAN BEING, I enjoy discovering "found" objects, and get excited about repurposing them. Yet, the reality is that I often end up not creating the time to do this, that, and the other step needed to complete my visions. So they don't always reach their exciting conclusions!

Once I looked in a drawer, and spotted an orange workman's glove I had tucked into a plastic pocket. What I didn't expect to see was condensation and mould. Whoops! Mouldy moments haven't stopped me from continuing to notice and gather more objects, but they have encouraged me to be more selective with them and more realistic with my projects. Also, mould can be beautiful too – it's all about perspective.

I am in good company with some of my favourite story characters. Goblins, dragons, and magpies also collect. They secretly scuttle, grab and store their treasures, sparking hope, visions, and dreams for their future. I find them inspirational.

At festivals like Glastonbury or Burning Man, too, incredible repurposed installations are temporary monuments for the event. Artists create remarkable exhibitions out of found objects. Waste and trash becoming treasure and enlightenment.

Perhaps we can learn from repurposing. Perhaps we can open our eyes and notice when someone else's trash is meant to be our treasure – treasure independent of others' valuation or affirmation, treasure that lights us up.

We can also remain open to discovering that what we thought was treasure, is now meant to be released, for discovery by someone new.

Finders' Keepers
by Elizabeth Papalia

Tramp, tramp, tramp
scuff, scuff, scuff
along they went.

Beady eyes flicking
this way and that
for another "found object"
Inspiring installations
sculptures
rickety towers of rubbish
soon to become art
transformed through touch and vision

Glinting, greedy eyes
gobbling up the pavement.
Sampling every morsel found:
taste buds alert, ready to notice
Notice what? You might ask
Lost, possibly forgotten,
objects with a future.

There!
A glove.
A pebble.
A crushed skeletal leaf.
A sock. A rock.
A photograph.
A...

Quick, hungry hands snatch up
their discoveries
stroking, touching, sniffing
dreaming of their purpose
imagining their new lives.
Finders' keepers, you see.

Story behind
A Moment in Nature
by Jen Blaxall

HAVING A DEEP CONNECTION WITH NATURE, and living and working in the heart of the New Forest, I offer nature therapy as part of my work. As clients simply stop and open their senses to their surroundings, they reconnect with their innate knowing, from which they evolved. This often has a profound effect on them as their pain starts to heal, and their emotions are released.

I don't need to be asked twice to go into nature and sit. It brings out my creative side.

Though I spend every day out in the beautiful New Forest, when I re-read this poem it takes me back to the moment I was inspired to write it, and to the deep, open-hearted, grounded, and calm sensation nature provides.

A Moment in Nature
by Jen Blaxall

Everything makes me smile, as so still I stand,
Dragonflies on the breeze and buttercup in hand.
I watch the forest unfold in the warmth of the day,
Mares sun their backs as their foals start to play.

The bracken gently shimmers in the shade and the light,
The heath thistle tempting the butterfly in flight.
Cows gently murmur to each other in their herd,
While deer lie in the shade, quiet and undisturbed.

Buzzards on the thermals repeatedly circle and call,
While clouds create images as they distort and reform.
As I sit here in nature amongst wonder and awe,
I am mindful, quiet and grateful for all.

Story behind
September Magic
by Jen Blaxall

I WALK IN THE NEW FOREST daily, and in every season I find joy and aspects I love. But September is one of my favourite seasons of all. It still has the feel of summer, but Autumn is waiting in the wings. Change is coming. The forest is thinking about letting go, but before she does, she delivers. Fruit and nuts are abundant, and all her wildlife gets busy!

I take my guidance from nature, and so, in my life, September is a time for foraging and thinking about what I want to change and let go of – before the winter solstice arrives.

September Magic
by Jen Blaxall

Walking the tight rope between two seasons,
Autumn strengthens as summer weakens.
Sun still dapples the leafy green forest,
While fruit laden boughs are ready to forage.

Bats still fly and reptiles bask,
But warmer drinks fill my flask.
The heathland warms in the mid-day sun,
But offers a chill as a shorter day is done.

Evenings draw darker, and the mornings wake later,
In the last few weeks of collecting butterfly data,
Dragonflies rattle along mint water streams,
And visitors leave with their holiday dreams.

Autumn is coming, the change can be felt.
The berries and bonfires can almost be smelt.
Fungi is fruiting, it's good to remember,
The best month for change is always September.

Story behind
Never
by Lori Michael

I HAVE A DEAR friend, a best friend, who is about to turn 70. He speaks of making plans to give away his belongings and shares with me what it's like to have outlived many of his friends. At 57 myself, I imagine there might come a time when I live without him on the planet. I think of the earnest plea in the Dylan Thomas poem: "Do not go gentle into that good night." I imagine myself asking my friend not to die… but that doesn't feel quite right. Then came "Never."

Never
by Lori Michael

I'd never ask you not to go.
Every day I think it, though.

So many I can take or leave.
I'd miss them, but I wouldn't grieve.

For you, I'd make a deal with God.
To keep you, I would give my all.

Maybe if I hold my breath
Or tie a string, we'll fend off death.

Or maybe you can bring me with you
To that bright new wilderness—

But if you go, and I must stay,
There will not be a single day
When my heart will not look up,
Expand, and reach as far and wide
As memory needs to bring you close.
Where I walk, you'll walk beside.

I'll feel you in the slightest breeze.
I'll show you every flower I see,
And every bird, and every tree.
I'll hear you laugh when children play.
We'll be together every day.

And when I go, I won't unwind
Until I you in Heaven find.
And there we will forever be.
Just me and you, just you and me.

Story behind
Nightfall
by Aidan Lazzarotto

I WROTE THIS POEM while sitting on a hill, staring out at the horizon with its noble sun and crisp blue sky. My dad had just died, and I had found out that morning by email…. Email. What a terrible medium for finding out your father has passed, and that you will never see him again.

My father and I had not spoken in nearly fifteen years. I had removed him from my life at a time when our relationship was hazardous to my well-being. My intention was always to include him in my future, and I had been working towards that goal in therapy. In fact, I had just written him a letter earlier that week. I am sad that I will never be able to read it to him in person.

Mourning is a natural human process of moving through our feelings and memories. It is a truly beautiful experience when we allow ourselves to be immersed in our feelings without judgement or shame. Mourning is the most intelligent vehicle for healing and equanimity that we possess. We can trust its reliable orbit, much like the sea of stars that circles overhead. If we allow our process of mourning to work its magic, without fear or interference, our sun shall rise again.

Nightfall
by Aidan Lazzarotto

The sun sets on a life.
A world goes dark.
Night falls.

The world that arises is not the same as before.
It is a world without you.
It is tomorrow without your smile.

The sun sets on a life.
Night falls.
Mourning comes.

Story behind
bones & flowers
by Lori Michael

WHEN MY MOTHER PASSED away, I knew her body would be buried at a cemetery near her home, alongside the bodies of my grandparents. It's a beautiful cemetery and I had been there before, but I sensed that, as close as I was with my mother and as much as I would miss her, I would not want to "visit her" there. Her life had been dynamic, filled with people and activity. I couldn't imagine going to what seemed to me such a somber place as a way of honoring her memory. This poem came as I thought of the ways I would remember her.

The irony is that some months later, I was taken by the desire to visit her gravesite. There, I had a most profound experience of connection with her, even carrying on a conversation with her. It was so lovely to be in a quiet place, surrounded by nature—especially the gorgeous trees and "big sky"—where I could focus undisturbed on her memory. As with some other traditions that I rejected at first, once I felt the freedom and desire to choose it for myself, visiting my mother's grave became something I wanted to embrace.

bones & flowers
by Lori Michael

yesterday i missed you in a different way,
but today i miss you from this café.

everyone went to that green place
to be closer to you.

i said i see you everywhere,
and so i didn't go.

you pull the lines out of me,
because you're so far away,

like the moon pulls on the deep, strong sea,
and makes the salty waves.

here, ceiling fans are turning, and outside the big window,
today's another brilliant day.

from where will i miss you next, i wonder?

not from that green place.

if i made up my mind to see you there,
i know i never would.

bones and flowers, stones and quiet
never could be my way to you.

instead, today, this minute,
i'll find you in someone's eyes --

and everyone i give love to,
that'll be me loving you.

Story behind
Cells of My Shadow
by Janis Vogel

THIS POEM IS ABOUT the non-linear quality of healing. Breakthroughs are made, and that is exciting. Then, if the ebb and flow of healing hasn't been accepted, when setbacks arrive, they can be devastating. The truth is that healing is a way of living, not a job to get done or a destination at which we arrive. And it is beautiful none-the-less.

Cells of My Shadow
by Janis Vogel

this cannot be happening
this old flight
this old fright
this old freeze
my sweet fawn
my new voice says
hello, pain
what are you trying to tell me?
I haven't heard yet
but I am patient
it takes time to coax
years of pushing through
out of
the cells of my shadow

Story behind
Oh Wild Wind
by Sian Boissevain

WILD WIND CAME TO ME after a retreat, as I hugged a mighty oak tree in the wind. During the retreat, our group had sipped oak coffee under this tree, and had bathed with its leaves. Just before writing this poem, I had tuned into the medicine of the tree, and had asked it to ground me. I had asked it for wisdom.

I love the oak tree. To me, it is the king of all trees. Tuning in to hear it speak was a grounding and profound experience.

The wonders of forest bathing are truly healing.

Oh Wild Wind
by Sian Boissevain

Oh wild wind blow me,
oh wise oak show me,
oh Mother Earth hold me.
Let my free spirit soar,
let my roots grow deep.

Oh wild wind,
sing me your song.
Oh wise oak,
tell me your story.
The answers lie within me.

The truth will reveal itself.
Bring me back to my heart,
the pulse of Mother Earth.

Story behind
The Light
by Helen Amery

IN MY COACHING EDUCATION, I was fortunate to have had a trainer who taught me early on what was most fundamental to successful coaching: coaching presence. Tools and techniques came second.

However, I believed this presence belonged to this body; that it was somehow mine, and 'something' that I – Helen –owned, created or controlled.

I never considered testing this belief. I never inquired into how that could be. It just seemed to be how it was. That is not surprising, given we're taught early in life that we are this body and this name. Later we're taught that other attributes, qualities, and faults are ours too. We're then taught, 'you're not very aware', or 'you're very aware', and we take that attribute on as well, as though it's yet another thing that belongs to us.

However, as my journey evolved from psychological to spiritual, I discovered that these beliefs I'd carried around simply weren't true. I am not fundamentally a body; I'm certainly not a name. I'm not even my attributes, qualities, or faults. In fact, the one thing that remained when I took everything away that I was not – the one thing that could not be removed, has never changed, and in fact isn't a 'thing' – is the pure fact of awareness. Presence.

Awareness: that which illuminates all experience, that which gives rise to all things, that which is the space of transformation, that which I am.

The Light
by Helen Amery

Transformation happens
in the light of awareness.
You are that light.
Shining, eternal, infinite. Light.
Losing sight of yourself
in your creative process,
you forget.
It seems to transform is impossible,
clouding yourself with yourself.
Till you remember
and remember.
And light is seen as who you are,
shining, eternal, infinite awareness.
You are the light.
Transformation inevitable.

Story behind
Dance of a Life Well Lived
by Julie Foubister

I WROTE THIS POEM after the death of a dear friend to metastatic breast cancer.

I had been contemplating what life would be like if it did not contain sorrow. My conclusion was that the avoidance of pain and sorrow is the avoidance of life itself. We cannot experience joy unless we've known pain, and we cannot experience love without also experiencing loss.

Dance of a Life Well Lived
by Julie Foubister

Strands sparkling bright
In all directions
Every emotion laced together
In beauty and awe
In pain and sorrow
My heart plucks every strand
In unison
The full spectrum vibrates
In the dance of a life well lived

CHAPTER 2

LOVE

"Love is the beginning of the journey, its end, and the journey itself."

DEEPAK CHOPRA

In a world full of differences, our need for love is a common denominator of the human experience. We seek it from the moment we arrive until our last breath. We spend our lifetimes experiencing it in all its facets and still have moments where its presence, loss, absence, and layers are indescribable. The poems in this chapter give lenses to the power of love.

Love, what a mystery, and what a gift.

Anjli Gheewala

Story behind
Love
by Gillian Walter

SOME TIME AGO, I was asked to do a strengths test by a colleague who was practicing working with strengths and shadows for a course. It was an online self-assessment, with results that arrived via email immediately upon completion. As I read the results, I saw that 'Love' was my number one strength.

I felt such disappointment. What use is that? Why couldn't I have useful strengths?! I mentioned this to the colleague, only half in jest, when we met to review my results. She helped me realize that it is precisely this love that is the foundation of my work as a coach and coaching supervisor. I now celebrate love as a multi-faceted, and often paradoxical force, that is found everywhere if we choose to see it.

Love
by Gillian Walter

It's in broken lenses that allow me to see,
It's in boundaries that set me free.

It's in glue that unsticks my tethers,
It's in storms that bring beautiful weather.

It's in getting it wrong that I understand
more,
It's in letting go that wins tug of war.

It's in silence that allows me to hear,
It's in giggles that evaporate fear.

It's in falling that opens our wings,
It's in giving that abundance brings.

It's in saying no that opens our choices,
It's in vulnerability that joins brave voices.

It's in cutting loose that brings us together,
It's in self-awareness that we know better.

It's an invisible force that helps me see,
I give it to you, when I give it to me.

Story behind
Go Where the Love Is
by Susana Rinderle

A YEAR AGO, I reached a stage in my healing where I recognized I was trying to get love from people and places that simply weren't able to provide it – no matter what I did to try and "earn" that love. In this futile striving, I was re-enacting my childhood neglect. This poem is a reminder that others' inability to see me or love me isn't because of my unworthiness or lack. I'm not to blame. I am worthy and enough. When I heal my shame and story of brokenness, I go where love exists. I go where love is given freely. I no longer try to "squeeze water from a stone."

Go Where the Love Is
by Susana Rinderle

Go where the love is.
Do not hate
the funny shape
that is you.

Contorting yourself
into some twisted turmoil
changes nothing
but your own happiness,
proves nothing
but how poorly you regard
your true nature.
They have no right
to dictate or mold
your final form.
They have not earned it.

Remove that stifling mask.
You can't breathe.
You know better.
Experimentation is for the young.
You're too grown
for lies
and wasted sunrise.

Know this:
It matters not
how you throw the pearls.
Not
how many
how far
to where
or when.
It's got nothing to do
with your timing, technique,
or delivery.
It's not you.
The problem
is they are
swine.

You can shout louder and longer –
they cannot hear you.
Your hoarseness is in vain,
for they do not
have ears.

Give up your useless laboring.
Drop your arms
Stop striving
Change the channel
Inflate your lungs.

Go where the love is.
Stop trying to make them
love you,
or make yourself
their type.
Stop insisting
on what they cannot give.
You will fail.

Instead,
Embrace your gorgeous needs
Celebrate your worthy longing
Un-pretzel and re-discover
the sublime shape
that is you.

Go
Where
The Love
Is.

Story behind
The Choice to Love
by Rama Krishna Rao

"*THE CHOICE TO LOVE*" is a poem of appreciation for the courage and vulnerability that come with the choice to love and be loved. Eleven years ago, when I wanted to take that leap and be married, my parents who were very traditional, said no. My decision to marry my wife despite my family's objections was a brave one, one that wasn't easy. But, in the end, our years together have been worth it, and I am grateful for the choice I made to love and be loved.

The Choice to Love
by Rama Krishna Rao

Loving and being loved is no small feat
It takes courage, trust, vulnerability to complete

The choice to love can be a challenge to make
But it's a risk worth taking for our hearts to wake

Love is a gift, if you take a chance
It can heal wounds and offer a new dance

Love is an investment of heart, mind and soul
It's a journey that can make us feel whole

And while loving and being loved can be hard
It's a choice that can bring joy to every heart

So choose to love and to be loved
It's a brave decision, worth all in the end

Story behind
Anniversary Poem
by M Bukowska

I WROTE THIS POEM in 2019 in the middle of a supermarket aisle. It was my parents' 50th wedding anniversary, and I had just texted my dad, asking him how they had managed to stay together, through all their trials and tribulations, for over fifty years. He wrote back that they were "eco-people" – they fixed what was broken, and went for real things, not single use disposables. Then he added "Besides, I think I really love your Mum".

His short and simple answer humbled, touched, and inspired me so much that I had to write then and there, in the middle of a very uninspiring and unsentimental supermarket.

This poem, from my book "BrokenHearted Wisdom", will always remain one of my favourites. It is a tribute to the two extraordinary people who gave me language, and who, despite our not always easiest dynamics, continue – to this day – to teach me what love is, and what love isn't.

They remind me to not settle for anything less than what love is.

Anniversary Poem
by M Bukowska

In this disposable world
of hook-ups and throw-aways
His shaking hand
reaching out for Hers…
Their love
as wrinkled as they are
battered by time
dented by life
Enduring
like their resolve to stay alive
And just like Her smile
-ethereal
And like the twinkle in His eyes
-eternal
Their Love

Story behind
I Memorized the Algorithm
by Jennie Linthorst

SINCE MY MOTHER'S EARLY death when I was twelve years old, my thoughts of mortality have shaded my moments of joy. Now as an adult, this early imprint shows up as an intricate dance between happiness and fear of loss, especially in my relationship with my husband. The more I love him, the more I fear the loss of him.

I Memorized the Algorithm
by Jennie Linthorst

There it was like an evil game of peekaboo
in sweet silence after making love.
A flash that my husband might die.
Our mortality jumps out at me in the news,
folds into creases of fresh sheets,
drives away with my son each morning.
Even sunlight after all this rain feels ominous.
I keep grief beside me as my wingman,
knowing happiness won't stick around.

Grief and I found each other
in dark corners of my childhood
as I circled unspoken uncertainty
during my mother's cancer—
surgeries, treatments, holding our breath
through spans of remission.
I stood in my kilt and saddle oxfords
to hear she was gone,
awake now to the game of probability.
I memorized the algorithm.

I want to be that couple
holding hands at ninety,
shuffling around our block at sunset,
layers of our lives thick inside us.
I search for the exact equation—
healthy living divided by family history,
multiplied by bad habits, plus inherent risk,
equals one of us might die too soon.

I collect comfort found in the in-between.
My cheek on his shoulder,
a kind glance from across the room,
his hand on my hip—armor
against the game of chance.

Story behind
The Lovedandlost
by Frances Simpson

I WROTE THIS POEM after the death of my dear friend's husband. His funeral was a beautiful humanistic gathering, set on stunning clifftops overlooking the sea.

I was moved by both the outpouring of love for him, and the agonising pain of my friend, and reflected on the exquisitely painful cost of love, when it is finally, inevitably lost.

Having just come out of a relationship, I had previously decided that I would not take such a risk again – until I experienced this immense love and loss. It changed my heart. From this reflection of love and loss, I wrote this poem. Well, it wrote itself.

The Lovedandlost
by Frances Simpson

Better to have loved and lost, they say,
than never to have loved at all.
But what do they know, with their pithy platitudes?
What do they know of *lovedandlost*'s boundless abyss?
The screaming jaws of grief so sharp,
It tears holes in the souls of the *lovedandleft*.

Surely preferable is the *hatedandlost*;
the demise of a demonic husband
and a lifetime of brutality.
Bruises and scars that marked
our days, weeks, months
of incarceration.
Then surely this loss is not bitter, but sweet,
A nectar of liberation.

Or even, *indifferentandlost,*
the safest option of all.
Terse exchanges of data, binbags and bills paid.
Mutual monotony, a shelter from
the twin perils of loneliness and love.
This loss greeted with a nod, a shrug,
trepidation at unsolicited solitude.

But love, this gaping flesh wound
exposed to the elements,
with its risks, its fragility, its ambiguity,
the inevitability of its loss –
I have seen this love
as the ultimate act of valour,
with rewards too priceless to quantify.
To have seen, known, delighted in another
is indeed to really have lived.

The *livedandloved* can neither be
the *lovedandleft,* nor the *lovedandlost.*
So I agree. It's better to have lived and loved
than never to have loved at all.

Story behind
Red Love
by Anjli Gheewala

MUCH OF LIFE REMAINS a mystery. How do we feel deep love, regardless of our differences? How can we see the silver linings when life events are difficult to accept? Why would a mother's timeline be longer than her children's?

Life unapologetically lends us grief as well as glory, while we borrow time.

This poem was inspired by the legacy of my grandmother, Ramkuverba, and family events. Ramkuverba's wisdom continues to guide the women she embraced as her own. Her daughter-in-law, my mother, is one of these women.

This poem has a mention to Rumi's poem *The Field*.

Red Love
by Anjli Gheewala

Who am I to write this? I am no one.
I am in the Field, the Field is in me.

The Field says: *take the fire of death*
and strike it with love. I dare you.

Blood whispers: *know where you come from.*
Remember that blue will come,
blue will go.

Never will your heart glow red,
when not in flow
with your thread.

To be in flow is to know
the truth of what came first.
What came first was you and me, and Mother.

You and Me, our love, and the Field.
See? Our love came first.
It came before the blue.

No one makes the case,
it is in shadow, unclaimed.
If you go, I go. If I go, you go. And so, we go.

The irony no one will see is this:
The fire of death circles the fire of love
because love came first.

Love has an order.
Blood makes its case:
The only real case, the only real order, is the
order of love!

Don't get lost in the blue.
Be found in the Field.

In any case, sooner or later, there will be a
fire,
and you will have to strike it red with love.

Story behind
A Gateway Beyond Us
by Aidan Lazzarotto

SOMETIMES WHEN MEETING PEOPLE, I am moved by the essence of their spirit and their work. Such was the case in a recent conversation with a grief counsellor. As we explored our shared values, we noticed that we both engage our work from a similar philosophy of practice, one that values the innate well-being of the human mind.

There is a beauty and simplicity in how we are made. Much like a compass, all of us possess a thinking-feeling system that shows us the path our mind is walking. It lets us know when our thoughts have become repetitive patterns leading to joy or pain. This early-warning system shows us the quality of our thinking. It is evidence of the kindness of our design.

Grief is a part of this system. It highlights the many unseen parts of ourselves that need attention, tenderness, and care. It is the most graceful and purging sadness we possess. And its many stages become basecamps for brave adventurers seeking to summit life's peaks.

A Gateway Beyond Us
by Aidan Lazzarotto

Grief as a shadow
where my life ends
a magic or darkness
in which light bends

Grief as a gateway
to love and lust
to birth and triumph
to bones and dust

Grief as a nomad
who comes and goes
a passage through which
all of life flows

Grief as a wisdom
from my own heart
a place that I stand
when all seems dark

Grief as a stranger
Grief as a friend
Grief as a canvas
to help hearts mend.

Story behind
Hand in Hand – a Facebook post
by Rona Rowe

A COLLEAGUE POSTED A PHOTOGRAPH of Facebook – a close up of her holding her elderly mother's hand. She was visiting her in a care home for the first time in months, shrouded in PPE as the rules required. Her mother was lost in dementia, and this was the first touch between them, – through a barrier of blue plastic. I felt both the sadness and the significance of the moment.

The pandemic was a terrible time for people who had loved ones in care homes. I wanted to reach out to my friend – to acknowledge the love and longing in her photograph.

Hand in Hand – a Facebook post
by Rona Rowe

for Janet and her mother
15 March 2021 Covid lockdown
the day after Mother's Day

A lifetime of touch
encased in tissue paper skin,
every line
a moment of knowledge
etched into the landscape
of her particular life,

Diminished now
she may be,
dimmed by the passage of time,
and yet here you are
with her still,

And all that she is
and once was,
lives on
in the hand
that you hold.

Story behind
A Selection of HAIKU
by Richard Tyler

IN JUNE 2021 AS I planned my 50th birthday and dreamed up some big adventures, I failed to close the loop and agree my exciting plans. On December 7th that year I was handed my next adventure; Stage 4 Mantle Cell Lymphoma. A rare cancer that if I had no treatment, left me with just 3 months to live. Aggressive chemo ensued as myself and my family hunted around to pick up the pieces. Everything that we knew was thrown up into the air. My belief of 'I don't get cancer' was blown to pieces.

Months passed. May 2022 saw me in hospital for a bone marrow transplant; 4 weeks in one white hospital room, total isolation and then a following 3 months of home isolation. So, with all this time available, my heart was bursting to be creative. I discovered haiku. I started playing around with them when I was having my transplant. Don't ask me why! I had never heard of them but liked the neatness of them. They had a simple structure. Sometimes life inside my head can be overwhelming and noisy. These short poems hold me to something neat and tidy. Haiku is a Japanese form of short poetry: three lines, 17 syllables in total, taking the form of 5-7-5.

We are all living in times that weigh heavy on our hearts. There is little escaping the grief, sorrow and sadness that we bear. I have felt supported by my own capacity to write; putting pen to paper (not fingers to keyboard – it feels different) has allowed me to gently lay down my luggage.

My hope is that these haiku offer you some tenderness. It feels vital that we all remind ourselves that we are enough. More than enough.

A Selection of HAIKU
by Richard Tyler

i see in your eyes
what you won't see in yourself
someone who's enough

soul softly whispers
as it beckons me closer
let go I've got you

you might miss the fact
that although I appear brave
i quiver inside

Story behind
The Plumb Line
by Hélène Demetriades

ONE EVENING, AFTER I had massaged my father's swollen feet and his aching 105-year-old shoulders, and had helped him to get ready for bed, he thanked me and blessed me for 'protecting him'. My father was emotionally and physically abusive to me as I was growing up and hearing him 'bless me' was an altogether new and startling experience. It felt ironic that as a child I had felt largely unprotected by him. That night I had a powerful dream in which my sleep consciousness recognised a 'plumb line' between us. It was a symbol for the energy of love and spiritual intelligence that held and grounded us both in a field much larger than our separate self-identities, and which was now allowing for a deeper communication, even communion, between us.

The Plumb Line
by Hélène Demetriades

Father, I lift your thinning thighs, nudge
down your trousers, peel off your socks,
slide over satin skin, tenderised
by your ancient flesh.

Tonight in our goodbyes you stutter,
B-b-bless you for protecting me.

In the early hours I wake,
words flooding my mouth:
It's not me, it's not me
the safe-keeper,
it's the plumb line between us.

Story behind
The Night Spirit Spoke
by Sharon Strimling

POETRY HAS THE CAPACITY to speak beyond the intellect, to convey an understanding that can only be felt. For that I am especially grateful in sharing this story, which intellect could only diminish. So I won't say any more about the experience, but instead will share two insights that emerged over time.

First, I came to see that this experience made me no more or less special than I had been before, no more or less special than anyone else. That may seem obvious, but at the time, with a load of insecure thinking and a pesky desperation to be special, I had been heartbroken as the "specialness" of my experience faded. I came to understand that "Bring it. Now" was a call for all of us to come out from behind our shame, our desires to be better, and any illusion that we are not already exquisite and perfect.

Second, as beautiful as the experience was, when life next brought me to my knees, the power of it felt lost. That agony delivered a powerful gift – a reminder that experience comes and goes, and that revelation lands in our hearts, not to stay, but to remind us of its source: an infinite creative space of love.

Any experience, however mystical or spiritual, is not who we are. If we think it is, we will forever be looking for ourselves in our next spiritual high, or clinging to our last one, as I was. We will look right past the far more exquisite truth and "specialness" of who we already are.

The Night Spirit Spoke
by Sharon Strimling

We talked,
you and I, all night.
My heart asked, and you answered
every question.

You never tired of my endless
why's, how's or what's this?
You never said *enough for now,*
that's all, or *you need to sleep.*

You never said
You are one of many.
I have others to think of.
No, you gave me everything.

You played for me
all night, showing me
gossamer threads of light,
sketching for me the soft mesh

of heaven and earth,
form and formless,
us and you.
You held my shoulders,

eyes on mine, face to my face,
and uttered your only words
of our image-filled night:
Bring it. Now.

You shook my shoulders
as only Love can,
told me to be
exactly who I am,

come out from hiding
as only I can.
And I – only ever
meaning *all of us*.

At some point, I fell to sleep,
then woke with eyes of opal,
stunned by our seen world of sunrises,
flowers, births, and forests,

beauty almost unbearable.
Even more so, your unseen,
your perfect invisible.
You showed me to your door,

green ivy draped
down its cherry frame,
sunshine soft on my skin
as I walked through.

I played in your world of beauty,
did summersaults in your safety,
flips that could no longer break me,
reveled in your feeling of forever.

Until it faded, forever.
Until it seemed our night, yours and mine
was just a story, and never a forever.
I hated you for that.

You deceived me!
I stormed at your door,
now closed and locked,
wailed outside

wondered
argued, raged
until collapsed on your doorstep
I looked inward, and saw.

The beauty you gave
was never this story,
this declaration of itself,
a thing to be kept, a thing to be lost.

It was never a belief, a faith, an idea,
never a possession to grasp.
Things are things, and things fade.
It's the love that births them that stays.

We talked, you and I. All night.
You spoke in images
and three perfect words:
Bring it. Now.

Story behind
I Create a Cloak of Wonder
by Alison Smith

THIS IS A POEM ABOUT CREATING, and the power of a poet to create a world where the reader/listener can feel themselves. It is about the power of voice to bring beauty, truth and love. Its message is 'To wonder is to love,' and that to wear the cloak of wonder is to dress in the poet's garb and walk the walk of the creator. I hope this poem evokes the exhilarating force of poetry as a means of accessing the field of limitless possibility, the 'field beyond right and wrong' of which Rumi wrote.

I Create a Cloak of Wonder
by Alison Smith

"Love without trust is like a river without water."
– Harbhajan Singh Yogi

Today I will create a cloak of wonder.

I will sit patiently in an armchair by the window,
cup cold tea in my hands,
dream first
of peacock feathers with bold turquoise eyes,
dilated pupils above a green hill far away,
and a smiling cat, yes a smiling cat,
for starters.

But so many things are wondrous, like
geese flying unseen in the dark to the lake,
that bare-backed man between palm trees gazing,
dancers painting waves with delicate strokes,
two bright parrots flutter in an open gilded cage.
How to choose?

I place that wistful man, sit him atop a giant book.
There are mountains towards which he looks,
And there is sun,
And some trees in mist.

And there is a very last curlew, picking its way
along a river to the sea,
there is the future, a star in the hand
and the star is a paintbrush,
the star is a pen, but the voice...
the voice is a meteor shower love-song.

And only then do I arrive at the scene,
my feet sinking into some remembered warm sand.

And I place this cloak of wonder across my
shoulders,
I take my love and my trust, open my throat
and I walk.

Story behind
The Sea
by Tracey McEachran

IN JUNE 2021, WHILE WORKING FROM HOME, I began a new routine of going to the beach at low tide to swim. I had never before been a water person, but had always been fascinated by the older women I saw swimming in the sea year-round. Even though I thought they were slightly crazy, I admired them. Forty years later, I began to do the same. I went to the sea every day I could and didn't stop when the summer ended.

And so it began. In October 2021, I purchased a beach hut to ensure I could have my own space from which to swim, sit and listen to the sea. Now if I go to the water – any time of year – I feel a strong need to submerge myself in it. It calms my soul and restores my energy.

How could I not write a poem about this immersive experience that feeds my soul?

The Sea
by Tracey McEachran

Why the water?
What is the draw?
I feel compelled to be there
floating in the swell

My skin tingles
comes alive
the salt in my nostrils
the taste on my lips

The sea is the great leveller
I could be rich, or poor
human measures, there is no score
When we take to the sea
we are insignificant.

But somehow
the power of the water
speaks to my soul
of who I am
I feel significant
I am whole

As I move through the sea
the force of the water
the crash of the waves
meet me as they meet the shore.

Then here, a gentle swell
water dragged over the seabed
a beautiful sound
Movement on the surface
in time with the deep
a constant dance of moon and
tides

For a moment I join
until I feel my skin no more
have to make for the shore

Leaving this majestic entity
I'll sit and watch
Sensations return to my body
Grateful
Humble
Enriched

Story behind
Home
by Anna Springett

I WROTE THIS ON THE 31ST DAY OF LOCKDOWN in the UK. Those first few weeks and months of pandemic lockdown were, for my family and I, a relief from the fullness and business of life. We took time over baking, art and crafts, and our daily walk, alongside the schoolwork and professional work that somehow did not need many hours in the day.

Those few months gave me the opportunity to really and properly slow down, in a way that I had never experienced before. I was writing, journaling, doing yoga, and gardening many times throughout each week – all the soulful activities that support me in staying sane and connected to myself in normal times. This extended period of time-spaciousness seemed to open things out, allowing air and light to flow into the places that were forgotten: I found myself again, and it was a nourishing, healing period that sustained me over the months ahead.

Home
by Anna Springett

I'm playing catch up with myself
In slow motion, gathering.
I've stopped here:
And the rest of me is bumping like dominoes.
Until I tumble together in a comfortable, unfamiliar rest.
Hello me, I say, in wonder.

I fold myself together in apology
Finding where the missing parts belong
The borrowed make-believe and best attempts discarded
With bemused relief: I always knew.
The greatest love story
The coming home.

Story behind
I Love You For Who You Are
by M Bukowska

SOME YEARS AGO, in a span of just a few days there were many conversations with friends. And there was a theme: the people I cared about very much worried that if they shared what was going on in their heads, I'd think they were "too dark or "too crazy". They feared I wouldn't love them anymore. This hit a nerve.

It reminded me that at one time or another, we all feel vulnerable and need to be reassured of our value, and receive unconditional acceptance and love. This poem was my best way to let my friends know that I saw the light and the darkness in them; the good, bad, and the amazing. I saw it all, and accepted it all, and loved them for them, no matter what.

I Love You For Who You Are
by M Bukowska

I love you for who you are,
for all your broken pieces
and the light that you shine through the cracks
not even knowing that you do.

I love you for the things that I see in you,
your smile, your courage.

I love you for all that you try to hide
your sadness, your vulnerability,
your madness that makes you climb the walls.

I love you for all the times you reach out to me
and I love you for honouring your own aloneness.

I love you when you stand in your light,
and when you are facing your shadows.

I may not see all of you,
though I see more than you think you show.

But I love all that you are,
your light, the sparkle in your eyes,
those untamed demons
that even you didn't know they lived in you.

I simply love you for... You.

CHAPTER 3

ACCEPTANCE

"Pain is inevitable, suffering is optional"

THE DALAI LAMA

Acceptance enables us to bridge the gap between our expectations and reality. Acceptance transcends our lower consciousness, allowing us to look up and take charge: we are not in control of life however we can choose how we react to it. Acceptance allows us to grieve our losses and find new meaning in our lives; it reduces our suffering. The poems in this chapter are written from the perspective of each poet walking their own path towards acceptance.

Sarah Moores

Story behind
Home
by Todd Roache

TO ME, THIS POEM speaks of the transcendence that can blossom from radical acceptance.

Acceptance of paradox. Acceptance of mystery. Acceptance that we can't know. And acceptance of ourselves: the good, the bad, the ugly.

And under all those layers of acceptance, what is left?

Love.

Love as the page on which we are all written.

Love as the energy from which we are made.

Love as the arms we fall into, within ourselves, when we let go of naming, blaming, and shaming, and just... be.

Home
by Todd Roache

I am broken
Yet whole

I am flawed
Yet perfect

I am despicable
Yet divine

I am unforgivable
Yet already forgiven

I am made of darkness
Yet created by light

I am all wrong
And yet

All right

And when in a cold and lonely abyss
As fear and shame condemn my dark

Sparks of grace burst into flame
And call me by my truest name

Love

You are always

And can only ever be

Love

Story behind
That Quiet Revolution
by M Bukowska

THIS POEM, STARTED MANY YEARS AGO and rewritten many times, in a way, journaled my growth of learning personal boundaries. On that bumpy road to self-acceptance, I learnt it was ok NOT to take an active part in other people's dramas. It was ok to say 'No' even to my nearest and dearest, and to walk away, if staying meant compromising myself, and that at times it was healthier to love from a distance.

My most important realisation of that time was that it was safe and necessary to take care of me, and to offer myself the love and acceptance I was so readily and unconditionally giving to others. The wisdom I've since been sharing with friends, colleagues, readers, clients: It really is safe for YOU to love Yourself.

That Quiet Revolution
by M Bukowska

That quiet revolution,
When You don't fight or scream,
But gently walk away
From the labels
That others stuck on You,
When You leave the drama behind,
And no matter who tries to pull You back,
You walk away,
From them too,
That silent rebellion of Your soul,
When You just let go
Of all that no longer is You,
All that drowns Your soul,
You walk away
From the prescriptiveness of Your society,
From all the should-s, and don't-s...
You just walk away,
And as You start breathing in the freedom,
You just know –
It is safe for You to love Yourself...

Story behind
Everyone
by Patricia Ahern

I WAS ONE OF MANY who operated on autopilot to please others, often with self-sabotaging behaviour. At some point, I had developed an automatic "yes" to everyone. Through my coaching journey I realised so many of us, out of a need for acceptance and/or a fear of rejection, say yes. We say yes over and over, with little or no regard for ourselves. Our lack of self-care can lead to break down, resentment and burn out.

Having high empathy is a strength. But I am now aware that when strengths are overdone or overused, they can become our greatest weaknesses and hinder us in reaching our potential. It is important to remember that we cannot pour from an empty cup.

Along my self-development journey, I read this: 'When you say yes to someone, make sure you are not saying no to yourself'. I regularly remind myself of this to ensure I don't revert to autopilot. Our "yes" is never about everyone else. It is about us, and our relationship with ourselves.

This poem speaks also to my realisation that it is not others' responsibility to think of me; it is my own. My wellbeing and self-care are my responsibility, and only I can set and keep my boundaries. The power is not in whether we say yes or no, but it's in our conscious capacity to choose.

Everyone
by Patricia Ahern

She gave so much of her to everyone
her body heart mind and soul
leaving not much for herself,
so could she ever feel truly whole.
Her beautiful heart torn apart so young
by someone who thought they knew best
the pain she felt from not deserving
she buried deep within her chest.
Her kind compassionate love
outwards she did bear
but for herself she did not
dare to even care.
So sad so young her heart did break
eventually her mind and body followed
from tears she didn't allow,
she quietly swallowed.
Invisible wounds deep within pained her
what could be done to heal them
what plan could be made
if, to rise from those scarred depths,
make changes, she was too frightfully afraid.
To try to try to try in vain to help
comfort her, to face her pain
but she would not allow it,
she felt she had nothing to gain.
So she kept on giving to everyone
and they just kept on taking
no one, realising all along
her gentle kind heart breaking
leaving not much for her own
bright, beautiful, worthy being
would she ever admit,
it's her self-love which needs freeing.

Story behind
A Familiar Stranger
by Ross Nichols

I DID NOT ATTEND my grandmother's funeral. A soldier in the British Army, I was living in Germany at the time, and was exhausted after an operational tour.

Many years later, while traveling abroad during university holidays, my younger son missed his own grandmother's funeral.

'Grandma, I will always love you and will miss you always,' the celebrant read aloud in his absence. As I heard his sentiments, my own delayed grief for my grandmother hit me. As I became fully present to my feelings, these two poems started to emerge. It was a complete surprise, as I had never written poetry.

This first poem is about identity, and a wakeup call to finding ourselves again when we've been lost. My wakeup call was on a grey, wet winter's day, a few months after leaving the Army. I was wandering around the house like a zombie, propped up on antibiotics for a chronic illness.

As I walked into the bathroom, I noticed a strange reflection in the mirror. 'Who are you?' I said out loud. I knew I'd been struggling, but it was then that I realised the depth and darkness of the hole I was in. I was no longer a soldier; and I realized that when I had handed in my ID card, helmet, and gas mask, I had handed in my identity; I had no idea who or what I was.

My confusion was exacerbated by the pain, fatigue, and misery of my illness, and I spent a year at the bottom of this black hole before I began my two-year quest for wellness. What I learned is shared in my second poem, 'On Being'.

These two poems are book ends to the most challenging chapter of my life.

A Familiar Stranger
by Ross Nichols

Two dull lifeless eyes look back at me,
A familiar stranger in my bathroom mirror.
I ask, 'Who are you?' They don't answer.
My sense of self is shattered.

Never have I felt so lost, alone.
Yet here I am, wherever this is,
Adrift with no anchor and no sails
Numb, in the unknown.

This is where my journey begins.

Story behind
On Being
by Ross Nichols

I DID NOT ATTEND my grandmother's funeral. A soldier in the British Army, I was living in Germany at the time, and was exhausted after an operational tour.

Many years later, while traveling abroad during university holidays, my younger son missed his own grandmother's funeral.

'Grandma, I will always love you and will miss you always,' the celebrant read aloud in his absence. As I heard his sentiments, my own delayed grief for my grandmother hit me. As I became fully present to my feelings, these two poems started to emerge. It was a complete surprise, as I had never written poetry.

This poem is about identity, and a wakeup call to finding ourselves again when we've been lost. My wakeup call was on a grey, wet winter's day, a few months after leaving the Army. I was wandering around the house like a zombie, propped up on antibiotics for a chronic illness.

As I walked into the bathroom, I noticed a strange reflection in the mirror. 'Who are you?' I said out loud. I knew I'd been struggling, but it was then that I realised the depth and darkness of the hole I was in. I was no longer a soldier; and I realized that when I had handed in my ID card, helmet, and gas mask, I had handed in my identity; I had no idea who or what I was. The experience of this moment is shared in my first poem, 'A Familiar Stranger'.

My confusion was exacerbated by the pain, fatigue, and misery of my illness, and I spent a year at the bottom of this black hole before I began my two-year quest for wellness. What I learned is shared in this poem, 'On Being'.

These two poems are book ends to the most challenging chapter of my life.

On Being
by Ross Nichols

What does it mean to be, not do?
How can you finally be more you?
How do you find a life you love?
How do you find a way to choose?

Questions, questions, are where it starts,
Questions simply, to open your heart.
Open your heart and let light in.
This is how your journey begins.

Is it so simple, simply to be?
Yes, but that doesn't mean it's easy.
Take your time to know yourself,
Listen and feel for your inner voice.

The road may be long and tough,
Yet this is a journey to love.
Love for yourself, love for others,
This is what really matters.

What's the secret, how do you start,
To find a way to open your heart?
Sit still and simply be you.
See what comes up and embrace it in full.

This is your way, your truth, your light,
It comes from within, no need to fight.
Yes, courage is needed to face your fears,
And facing them brings a power to heal.

So, let go of others' voices,
Simply be you,
It's your life,
Who are you?

Story behind
The Secret Sauce
by Todd Roache

IT HAS TAKEN ME a long time to discover and befriend some of my darker aspects. It's a journey I am still on, and perhaps will always be on. What I initially feared as monsters in the dark depths, even foes, turned out to be allies and essential parts of my whole.

Take one important cog out of a finely tuned race car and...? Take one animal out of the ecology of the woodland and...?

And so in this poem, I draw attention to a seemingly small dark/taboo/unwanted part, and muse on how once it's met, accepted, embraced, and integrated, the result can be a more complete, resourceful, potent you! (And me.) Another glorious team member added, with its own special skills to contribute.

And with that part 'in play', with that expanded inner team, what then becomes possible?

The Secret Sauce
by Todd Roache

That bit of you
You keep hidden
Because you think it's too fucked up
Too taboo

Hidden from yourself even
Not 'in play'
You might say

What if that's the secret sauce?

All those hopes and dreams and schemes
Half dying in your office drawers
What if they need that little spice…

That little something more?

Maybe it's just one percent, but still,
Like a drop of dye in water,
It changes the hue
Makes you more…
You

You say you're doing all you can
Every little thing
But if you're not 'all of you'
Then who is the one doing?
And is it the fullest 'doing'
You have yet to bring?

I'm not saying run down the streets
Shouting it out loud
(It is a 'secret' sauce after all)
But what if you let it into your
bloodstream
Accept it
Let it take its place...

Maybe then that 'dream'
Wouldn't be a dream at all.

Story behind
Facing Up To My Story
by Sarah Moores

MY STORY WITH THIS POEM is as old as time. It's about our belief that ageing makes us less beautiful. It's about how somehow, while we gain so much more of life by growing and learning, we lose something else in the process. Sure, youth may have more years ahead of it, but it doesn't have a head and heart full of where it's been, what it has seen, and what it has gleaned.

My work in progress is to recognise this. It is to appreciate my wrinkles, as marks that I have lived; appreciate my aches and pains, as reminders that I have taken my body places; appreciate that I might need more rest, as a sign that I have experienced so much. Each day of my life I grow – and I wouldn't swap a single day of my evolution for a body that hasn't lived.

So why is it so hard to accept its pattern on my face? Because my lines tell another story too. They tell the story of the sun I worship, and the self-blame of the lines that worship brought. And yet, I love the sun on my face! It makes me feel cherished, like I'm receiving love from above. So this is my next step. Can I accept the sun's imprint as an earthly manifestation of all that love? Can I allow my sun-filled lines to light up my face, shame-free?

Yes, I can. I start with a daily habit. I look expressly to remember what I have felt – the light and love in each and every emerging line.

Facing Up to My Story
by Sarah Moores

My skin glows, an English rose,
My eyes shine, twinkle bright
There's a blush to my cheeks, soft and rounded, a peach
Qualities time couldn't ravage

But I'm wondering now, as I raise furrowed brow
About age drawing lines without permission
The speech marks round my smile, I ponder for a while
Why did time have this face repositioned?

A happy or sorry tale, reading my lines like braille?
A roadmap of life on my face
Tracing fingers 'round my eyes, I smile to sympathise
My life force, shining through, in exchange

So here lies the clue, now I know what to do
Whenever criticism judges this old face
Accept the lines I could despise, allow what's inside to mesmerise
Self-love's a beauty, and a grace age can't erase

This portrait's taken time to master, and I wouldn't have had it any faster
A masterpiece like this, just takes time
Time for all my expressions, to create lines in succession
This face, my life's story, every stage

Each line a permanent tattoo, of what happened, me and you
An epic tale we just keep on growing
No greater beauty on earth, this gathering from birth
Lived experience, our front cover, open page

The heart of me which cares, my face now boldly shares
My insides now shine my expression
What more beauty could one behold, than one's story expressly told
On skin's canvas, lines of tales, as we age...

Story behind
Wild Animal Heart of Mine
by Gillian Gabriel

WILD ANIMAL HEART OF Mine is about letting go of comparison, hiding, holding back and fitting in. It's about me moving towards my heart's desire to be carefree, seen and true to myself. It's about this desire at last outweighing my fear and hesitation. Listening to my own wild animal heart pulled her up from my inner depths, and released me to run free.

There's a tipping point when our balance shifts from staying small and safe which hurts too much, to coming out. As Anais Nin wrote, "And the day came when the risk it took to remain tight inside the bud was more painful than the risk it took to blossom."

This poem was sparked by the ways in which women's wildness has been contained, and the freedom the Wild Animal Heart can claim.

Wild Animal Heart of Mine
by Gillian Gabriel

Wild.
Animal.
Heart.
Mine.

If I were **wild,** I really wouldn't care
Not careless, but, no worry of
"What will others think?"
I'd be spontaneous. I'd be free

If I were **animal,** I'd be raw to my bones
No mask for me
Natural and vulnerable
And open wide to see

If I were **heart,** I'd love unconditionally
Without fear of loss, I'd beat
In time to my own tune
A rhythm just for me

And if I were **mine**, I'd be all mine
And all me. Not you
True to the depths
No should, better, ought, must do

So, wild animal heart of mine
I can hear you, distant and sweet
Like a tribal drum getting louder, beat by beat
Faster and faster, at last we'll meet

We'll meet, you and I
We'll rise to the beat
We'll stamp our own feet
Wild animal heart of mine

Story behind
Thoughts
by Colin Cafferty

OUR THOUGHTS CAN BE scary. They can seem to control us, and we often identify with them. But we can choose to see them differently. We can create space for them to come and go – without attaching to them. This poem reflects my tendency to overthink, and my past struggles with anxiety and negative thinking. Coaching allows us to find new perspectives, and to develop healthier and more balanced relationships with our thoughts.

Thoughts
by Colin Cafferty

There's a dark place
I used to know so well,
Where spiders spin
Silken lies and sweet deceit,
Tangling thoughts
Once free to float
In the sky of my mind.

What if I learned to see
The vastness of the sky?
What if I learned to find
Dewy pearls on finest lace?
What if I learned to pick
The lock that jails my thoughts?
What riches I would have!

There's a dark place
I thought I knew so well.
Now fireflies dance
To the beat of new synapses
Across a vast neural web.
Step back and watch.
What a beautiful show!

Story behind
That Space
by Uphie Abdurrahman

BEHIND EACH JOURNEY of those suffering from complex trauma and childhood abuse is the longing and search for a safe space. It is not always easy to find one, given our difficulty to trust. That safe space can also be abstract, amorphous – a journey to identify as we heal. That longing for safety is expressed through this poem.

That Space
by Uphie Abdurrahman

There is a space
   quiet, comfortably cold,
   where my bones sprawl,
   their usual structure thaws into oil,
   languid and old;
   while joints unclench like cinnamon rolls
   on earthy, familiar wooden floors,
that feels exactly like contentment.

There is a space
   whose air is pastel, quartz, azure;
   my shell crumbles when it wants to,
   walls lose height, defences forget their meaning;
   exoskeletons mere mementos of a tortoise's inner peace,
   a grassy, familiar bed of earth...
that feels exactly like contentment.

There is a space
   whose breeze gently strips all masquerade,
   where my heady wannabes fade;
   inner monsters tame like mewling felines,
   scars iodine,
   souls crystalline,
   buoyant, familiar billows of clouds,
that feels exactly like contentment.

Lay me down,
   as my senses come crashing down...
   not in a casket, nor a bed of roses,
   but a mat woven from strands of
acceptance.

Lay me down...
    where all quality fails, and nothingness reigns,
    not a glorified pedestal,
    nor a palanquin of royals,
    but a hammock whose embrace has
few conditions.

There is a space...
    nowhere I would more lay down,
    than simply...
        in your arms.

Story behind
College Visiting
by Jennie Linthorst

FEW MOMENTS HAVE REQUIRED greater acceptance from me than letting go of my only child into the big scary world of college and beyond. This poem captures a moment we had on a campus tour in Arizona. It was on this hot summer day during the waning days of lock down, when I was faced with my own midlife crisis of a looming empty nest.

College Visiting
by Jennie Linthorst

Dry Arizona heat swallows our air.
We rest achy feet under a shaded tree,
sip from our water bottles.

I catch my reflection in a windowpane.
My yellow sundress clings to my middle-aged stomach,
a white braided belt has slipped down

like a sad bow on a wilted package.
I am now that woman of a certain age
touring a green campus

with my seventeen-year-old son.
I have read about these women in novels,
seen them on movie screens.

They live in a tangled forest of new beginnings,
weakened from years of parenting.
I notice a bloom of sunburn on my son's calf,

and his lips have grown red.
He'll never remember to put on
sunscreen.

We stroll past the campus commons
as students lounge and chat.
I pass another window,

my belt now turned a little to the side.
My husband mutters
something about lunch,

and all I can think about is ChapStick
and my son's empty chair
at our dinner table.

Story behind
Buoy
by Janis Vogel

ACCEPTING THAT WHICH PLAGUES us, allowing for that which disturbs our sleep, attending to that which sends knots to our necks, spins round in our head, is integral to our healing. It may be frustrating to stay with the feelings we would rather deny. We may want to hide, even if only from ourselves, or maybe especially so. But when we stay with ourselves, when we trust this process, we find where our knowing takes us.

Buoy
by Janis Vogel

Whatever you push down
bobs to the surface
again and again
wanting to be seen, validated
to be given permission to quiet down – sink
become a thing of the past
acknowledged
put to rest
not by being held under water
but by being lovingly tucked
in by the light of a bright moon

Story behind
The Visitor
by Leah Kaess

THIS IS A DESCRIPTION of a moment in time ~ a moment when sadness visits, a time when we wish it wasn't there. It's a reminder that emotions come and go; they're not who are. They're simply visitors, often unexpected and uninvited, who join us for a while. They're not our responsibility or our doing, and we don't have to try to get rid of them. In fact, they can serve as a reminder of the difference between the transient nature of what we feel and the eternal nature of who we are.

The Visitor
by Leah Kaess

The pain

runs through the atmosphere
and through my head

it doesn't seem to have a place
to land

what is sadness
when it's not specific?
it just is

it bubbles up
when it does

like soup coming to a boil
except that no one lit a fire under it

it often arrives without warning ~
we didn't order it
we didn't ask for it
we weren't expecting it

like an uninvited visitor
who shows up
at your door, knocks,
and lets himself in

he seems to know you,
to know everything about you

and yet you don't know him
not even
how he found your address, or
how long he plans to stay.

Story behind
The Movements of Sadness
by Uphie Abdurrahman

TO IDENTIFY EMOTIONS IS NOT EASY, especially emotions that have marinated for years, complex traumas bred since childhood and augmented by great events. 2019 was my rough year, with hauntings of sexual harassment, a constant trail of panic attacks, and depression. Writing was a part of the therapy that upheld me. I wrote constantly, in the hopes that being acquainted with these sudden emotions would someday help to settle them.

The Movements of Sadness
by Uphie Abdurrahman

1

My pen scrawls calligraphies,
  not of Happiness, but of Sadness,
    words that lilt as they sag
      under the lonely weight of suppressed verses.

2

For Happiness can be easily sourced
  through morning sunshine,
    or productive contribution's exuberant trot,
      through black coffee, a spoonful of honey,
        starfruit-infused water...
          through laughter, however feigned,
            for still facial muscles flex,
              through co-workers' radiant banter.

Because Happiness
  can be easily procured
    from Spotify's earworm-pop, bleeding bubblegum and chartreuse,
      from drag queen viral GIFs, shit-post memes, insta-poets,
        or random street-side munches packing surprise,
          from jellies & charred veggies,
            whiffs of wood glue,
              pills of fluoxetine,
                from ethereal gardens of vibrant batiks,
              gold-framed garudas perched on
            richly-oaked trees of life,
              deep blue Ramayanas,
                earth-colored mandalas and archways,
              plucked-blushes from this wardrobe,
            injected by a steroid of hues
              exactly to procure happiness.

Because Happiness
can be easily borrowed.

3
Yet, Sadness, its forgotten twin,
  the humiliated Yin in perpetual neglect,
    one who party-poops, shunned from social circles
      for conjuring awkward moments.
        Sadness is shushed by even trusted closests,
          the self-censorship cultivated to muffle
            outplaced screams by
              Debbie Downer.

Sadness darkens secretly
  like the unseen qualms of a court jester,
    like the festering gangrene of unrequited love,
      like lagoons at night
        that initially only reflect
          the blackness of the absence of light,
            till they hearken to prolonged saturnine,
              ink-black mars what used to be crystal.

Sadness, woes, grief, trauma
  play together without sound
    on a Four-Horsemen-of-the-Apocalypse carousel,
      which spins as they throw off,
        bit by bit,
          debris of a once-glimmering aura,
            becoming brittle, bone-white,
              ashening into dust,
                lingering into none.

Sadness is a lyre in one's mind,
  whose metastasizing, unstable frames are mercurial alloys,
    whose strings thrum a haunting melody
      of repressed past.
        Each note echoes every heartbreak life hands us
      in Facebook handles, Twitter trends,
    CNN, deaths of a friend,
  famine in faraway lands;
they ricochet

like funeral bells
  trapped in a box of mirrors,
    estranged by the world.

Sadness is a dusty tome left unsung,
  a yearning heart kept high-strung,
    a turbulent storm begging to be seen;
      they shyly open like springtime petals
        painting subsequent skies iridescent.

Sadness is Medusa,
  who might not be running amok with a head of snakes,
    had her heart not been petrified
      with heartbreak.

Sadness is a tenderness,
  an open wound beckoning a drop of ointment,
    a trembling skeleton asking for
      the softest caress.

4
I write about Sadness
  to tend to its sore flesh
              – even when the world alienates –
    before it dries
      into Numbness.

I write before Numbness
  renders meanings forgotten,
    and, all feelings,
      including manufactured ones
        fade.

Story behind
Speaking Stones
by Dearbhaile Bradley

I WAS ONE OF THE TRAUMA TEAM working with a bereaved family the night of the Omagh bombing (15th August 1998). Back then, I ran 'Chiron Counselling Services' training and supervising counsellors. I also worked for an Employee Assistance Programme and in private practice. I was working flat out, and I loved it.

But when I returned to work after the bombing, I struggled. It was difficult to adjust to the mundane after such a powerful experience. I decided that I needed to do something just for me. I signed up for a creative writing course for women, and squeezed it into my schedule. The other women attendees were all financially supported by their husbands and were ladies of leisure, now that their children had left home. Time and again, I found myself furious with their lack of awareness of what life was like for so many others.

I couldn't work out what to say, and was crushed by the crass reminder of privilege. After years of listening to people who entrusted me with their horrific pasts, this poem poured out. I wrote first in anger, then grief, then found myself in gratitude; in an awareness of the great privilege it was to have been trusted by these people.

Everything in the poem happened to someone who spoke with me. They are powerful people who deserve to be honoured.

Speaking Stones
by Dearbhaile Bradley

I

I have not spoken of secrets I've been told –
of the whispered mythologies of a thousand lives
touched briefly in the womb-room
where the voices come to break with me.

No, I have said nothing.
Childvoices speak to me
knowing the silence of
stoneselves.
Voices tripping up the stairs
to what lies buried in bedrooms.
Children with sad, silent eyes that say
'I suffer'.

I have not spoken of the things they could not say,
locked in their stoneselves.
I have told no-one the secrets
of the women and men
who have poured into me their memory.

'He said I could not say, not to anybody.'

Rather than shatter the world,
they held themselves together.
Turned to stone.

Low, sad, hesitant,
angry, loud, pained, shadowed,
all their voices live in me.

But still I have not spoken

of worlds where children are begged by their mother
to murder their father;
of little girls led by the hand into rooms
where fathers rape them;
of boys, bloodily weeping into toilets
afraid to let a sob escape them.

I have not said what I have learned
of dark rooms with lashing belts
and stumbling alcoholic breaths;
of waiting for hell to end in the coal bunker;
of hanging by one leg out a window
until submission;

of a baby born of night's screaming
that was by morning swallowed up
by night's knowing,
never to be spoken of again.

I know too much of this dark world
to know how I am to speak of it.

II

How can I soak up stories,
hold faith that speaking stones will heal them?
Stones swallowed so long ago
that live in throats waiting to be spoken?

I have taken this again and again to our green mother.
Wept upon her breast begging for help,
for the strength to soak up tears
as she soaks up mine
and never tires.

I have prayed

but I have not spoken.
For if I am to find a voice
I want it to be a voice of beauty.
I want to speak of iridescent dreams.
I want a voice that honours,
a muse-given gift of wordnets
capturing jewels of experience.

I have not spoken
because I know such ugly things.

Yet in the learning of these ugly things
I have seen beauty –
a healing light that glows around release.

Magic has flowed in these womb-rooms
where people birth themselves,
are born into voices that live and laugh
and speak of other things.

They leave me the fruits of their courage,
these tellers of ugly things
with their new-washed, fresh, tear-stained faces
where joy shines
as stoneselves are shed.

The petrified revive.
The old world ends.

They leave me their voices
stumbling on their stories.
Leave me their choked pauses.

They are my voices now,
my whispered mythologies.

And each one leaves before their new beginning
that I am left behind to imagine.

Story behind
In the Darkness
by Anna Springett

THIS IS A POEM about loss and grief, and the depths of pain and darkness that are often experienced in those hardest of times. In this particular story, I was still in a place of hurting when I began to realise I had closed my heart to some of lifes' most valuable insights and treasures. I don't think I can write about it any clearer here than I tried to capture in the poem – something of the rich tapestry of life and what it is to be human; how there may be things we can somehow embrace even in our most painful moments.

In the Darkness
by Anna Springett

I lost myself to hurt and pain
Allowed my soul to blister
I welcomed in the wounds and stains
Let go the role of sister
The darkness of the Other One
Poured in to flood my heart
It drowned out truth and light and hope
It blew my world apart
I sank into a cave so deep
I lost all sight of earth
And all life's other tragedies
Came down like shovelled dirt
It kept me there, held in this place
And knowness faded still
The weight of all these sorrows
My heart, my body, ill
I lurched into the underworld
A sick forgotten mind
The loneliness, the fear, the stench:
I stayed completely blind

Somehow, I found a tunnel out
I gasped – for light, and air
With grass-stains, muck beneath my
nails
Life's gleam no longer there
I grew into this unknown world
And found a normal pace
Of day-to-day and week-by-week:
A busy, harried pace
And kindness grew and healing came
and light began to dawn
A story formed to bridge the gap of
how I'd partly mourned
And yet the echoes still remain
Of mud and dirt and grime
And only now I recognise the treasures
left behind
They still remain there, underground
And buried deep inside
If only I'd had open eyes instead of
staying blind

There is adventure calling me
It echoes in the deep
A place where eyes accustom to
The mysteries in the keep
A darkness where the stars shine bright
A darkness that is filled
With jewels, diamonds, emeralds
A darkness that is stilled
I need to dive into the depths
To find these precious things
And only through the pain and grit
In places where wounds sting
You face your truest deepest place
Acknowledge depths of plight
You treasure them and hone them
And come back from the night

Story behind
Stillness
by Sharon Strimling

EVERY HUMAN I HAVE ever known has wanted peace. I find that miraculous.

Yet, as I explore peace, I am touched by the way it shows up in our full breadth of experience. We come to know the depths of freedom only against a backdrop of restriction, the power of love against a backdrop of loss.

This poem came out of a recent deepening of that understanding, where I saw myself about to flee a feeling that terrified me, stopped myself, and found the courage to be still.

What ensued was an exquisite beauty I would never have experienced had I chosen to chase refuge. It brought a richness and a healing I could never have imagined.

I was reminded, once again, that as frightening as any feeling may be, it is, first, harmless, then freeing, and ultimately exquisite and sacred.

I see more deeply that I am not the content of my experience, but the capacity for *all* experience. I am moved to live and play full out and to help others do so with me, held by the remarkable resilience and strength we share.

Stillness
by Sharon Strimling

I thought I couldn't take it -
this loneliness Sinatra crooned to me
in my kitchen, as I crossed
to silence him.

The ache of alone,
of separation, danced
too close to my toes.
But something caught me,

a curiosity, a craving
to listen, to feel, to live.
So, I held myself still,
arms squeezed at my sides,

and swayed to the aloneness
I thought I couldn't take.
Her weight pressed
into the soft of my chest.

Her gaze called heat
to the flush of my face.
Her force tested my body and mind
to let go the guardrails of familiar.

Her vitality became my partner
her dance became my love
her fullness became my life.
Then... as quickly as she arrived

she moved along,
to offer another her grace:
the grace of aliveness,
the fullness of being.

I swayed in my kitchen,
Sinatra still crooned,
and Alone, my sweet friend
remained -

in purity, in presence
in a flush of new knowing,
in powerful sensation
that does no harm.

Story behind
Progress
by Dearbhaile Bradley

THIS POEM IS BORN of my own experience of depression. There are times, because of the twists and turns on our paths, that we can't see the light that is rumoured to be at the end of the tunnel. If we can't see the light everyone says is there, does it mean our dark days will never end? The illusion of permanence can be convincing, and intrinsic to depression.

However, life is a labyrinth, not a maze. If we keep going, we will gain insight available through this powerful journey, and return wiser and more resilient. I, and people I've worked with, have found this knowing helpful when going through our darkest of days.

Progress
by Dearbhaile Bradley

In the labyrinth,
      not lost
   but
   treading
cautiously
      in the dark.
               Feeling for
      the thread,
   the friendly wall.
Slowly,
   trusting,
      knowing,
   this way,
      this way
         leads to
               light.

Story behind
Dear Fear
by Julie Foubister

I USED TO BE frightened of fear, and would run and hide from it. I became well-practised at living in the stress response of flight.

When diagnosed with cancer, my fear became too powerful and swift to outrun. Instead, I learned to sit with it, lean in, let go and let it have its say. As it turned out, I didn't need to run from it. It was ok. I was ok. Its lessons taught me, and I stopped the run. I came out of flight. That was the best thing I have ever done for my health.

Now, I encourage others to do the same – to sit with their fear and see what message it has to share. I invite them to sit, lean in, and let fear pass through – as it will.

Dear Fear
by Julie Foubister

Dear Fear,
I got so good at resisting you
Covering you in a blanket of denial
Gripping you tight; holding you in place
Whilst smiling at the world.

Dear Fear,
I didn't notice you sneaking out from under there!
Raising the alarm, gathering your allies
To shut me down
Stop me in my tracks.

Dear Fear,
You left me nowhere to go.
I finally turned in your direction to face you there,
Let go of my grip, couldn't hold you anymore.
There was nothing to do but hear.

Dear Fear,
You surrounded me and moved through me for hours.
But in the listening, you started to dissolve
Handing back, one by one, each part of me
I had lost to you.

Dear Fear,
The pain of that altercation, then letting you go,
Was nothing compared to holding you there.
I realised you're a traveller, with a story to tell
Not to be silenced or to be held.

Dear Fear,
I now appreciate your visits. Your calling card grip
Leads me to you, guarding a belief that isn't true.
You remind me to let go, to breathe,
and let you pass on through.

Story behind
Encrypted Love
by Basia Henderson

LIKE ALL OF MY poems, *Encrypted Love* was created through me rather than by me. I never feel entitled to claim full ownership.

The creation came from a deep place within my soul while I was in the middle of processing and healing from the breakup of my marriage, a time that was by far the most painful, yet insightful, heart opening and potent of my life. I craved solitude and silence, so I spent a lot of time in nature in deep reflection doing inner work. Surrender was my daily practice, which didn't always come easy. Yet I saw how transformative and healing it was to "let go and let God," as Dr Wayne Dyer would often say. This poem came from deep surrender.

I stopped questioning and resisting what I was going through, and understood that every person on our path is our greatest teacher, with an important lesson or message for us to understand and integrate. This is how we grow and wake up to our truest nature, which is pure love.

Having written *Encrypted Love*, I was of two minds if I should share it with anyone or not, as when I read it, I felt it didn't have a rhythm and seemed artistically imperfect. Is there such thing as perfection in art though? Maybe art in itself is perfection. And the message that came through was too good not to share.

Encrypted Love
by Basia Henderson

Remember the day life felt so good?
You thought it would last forever.

Sudden knock at your door
Kicks you out of your bliss.
A beautiful stranger was sent
To deliver a letter from God.

You open the door
Your heart full of hope.
But you read the letter
And your heart sinks.

Deep forgotten wounds
Rip open again.
You thought those days were over.
Yet the One who knows everything
Had different plans for you.

Don't dismiss the message
When it doesn't feel good.
Notice….
Did you have expectations?
What if you had none?

Don't shoot the messenger
Be grateful instead.
Get curious….
Could this be a love letter,
Encrypted for a reason?

Maybe you wouldn't pay attention
If it was too obvious,
Too easy.
Have you noticed
How we like to work for it?

Don't resist.
Open your heart even more.
Receive.
Be with it.
Feel.

See each thought for what it is,
Just passing clouds
While you are the sky.
Can you feel
That nothing is real?

Watch how things turn in an instant:
Pain into beauty,
Wounds into love,
Noise into silence,
Control to surrender.

Of course you can choose
To return to sender,
Opt out of the miracle.
Before the work is over
Return to your seeming bliss.

But know that one day
Another messenger will be knocking on your door,
And another...
And another...
Until you receive the message with grace.

There is no timeline
It's never too late.
You have eternity
And you have this moment.
They are the same.

You choose.

Story behind
Change
by Gillian Walter

I WAS IN A BEAUTIFUL PLACE, sharing a practice with two wonderful colleagues and friends in a 'location, location, location' space. Everything in the garden was rosy – until it wasn't. Both friends passed in two unthinkable disasters, leaving me colleague-less and office-less.

I tried to move forward, but letting go of them both seemed impossible. I pulled myself together enough to try to hold onto our space, but simply couldn't make it work alone.

I had to let go. And with support from my supervisor, I was able to. When I chose to start again, my colleagues' legacies and gifts helped build the foundation of my new practice. Their memories and lessons supported my decisions, and their gifts appeared as I was ready.

I love my new coaching space now, more than ever. And I know that this safe space for my clients has nothing to do with its four walls – but rather the hearts, love and connections that built it.

Change
by Gillian Walter

I have seen an era changing
I have watched as new seeds grow
I've held my breath through sleepless nights
Now there's something true I know

Change is the only certainty!
Love or hate the status quo
Hindsight offers no umbrella
When I really *should* have known

Clouds of change cast daunting shadows
In hidden corners of dread
For those who watch and wait in fear
So I consider this instead

I'll change the things I know I can
Choose to revel in the storms
Sing grateful songs to what is now
Greet each rainbow as it forms

Invite the special scent of rain
To water seeds of today
Welcome curiosity in and
Put my umbrella away.

Story behind
My Coaching Journey
by Kate Jenkinson

STRUCTURED COACHING AND DEVELOPMENT can get you so far. In the coaching world, GROW stands for Goal, Reality, Options and Way Forward. It's a common, results-focused coaching model that a person can use on their own for simple issues. When feeling stuck or trying to choose between known options, GROW can be useful.

However, as any model, it has limits. What if you are very unhappy or frustrated, and you need something to change, but aren't sure what? It's then that GROW isn't as powerful as something much deeper: finding what makes your heart sing.

How do you find that? You can start by asking yourself these questions: When do I lose all track of time? When don't I need to motivate myself – because I love what I am doing? If I put my heart's desire at the centre of my life, what would I change?

When I asked myself these deeper questions, I moved house, set up my own coaching business and immersed myself in the Spoken Word Community. Everything changed.

Finding our heart's flow with questions like these can open us up to so many more opportunities. Though, as I discovered, it may require something greater of us: to let go of other people's expectations. But what is our heart's song worth?

My Coaching Journey
by Kate Jenkinson

I started off with grow
and ended up with flow
and no
it's not an acronym

it's finding out
what makes your heart sing
where your soul needs healing
helping you find your
                    centre

from flow
anything is possible
but you've got to let go
of other people's othering

Story behind
As the Leaves Fall
by Gillian Gabriel

AS THE LEAVES FALL is a poem about how the form of life is always changing. It's about the seasons, the circle of life, and how I can hold the bittersweet – pure joy and pure sorrow – at the same time. I guess it's a paradox. Some things can be one thing AND another – which shouldn't make sense, but does. This poem is about our highs and lows, ups and downs, and life's yo-yo experiences that come and go. And it's about how that can break your heart, and be beautiful at the same time.

I always thought I was a bit strange, feeling a wave of grief as autumn begins. While others seemed to only be in awe at the wonderful colours of changing leaves, I used to think there was something wrong with me because I felt a damp cloud settle alongside the glory. I have a similar feeling on New Year's Eve as one year ends and another begins.

Now I really appreciate my state of bittersweetness, like sweet and salty popcorn. I am grateful that I get to experience both the pain and the beauty. I read Susan Cain's book 'Bittersweet' and realised it's a part of who I am. Susan explains bittersweetness: "It's the recognition that light and dark, and joy and sorrow, are always going to coexist, and that's what life is. And it's an awareness of passing time. An awareness of the impermanence of life. But it's also a kind of a piercing joy at how incredibly gorgeous and beautiful life is." – Susan Cain in Brené Brown's podcast Unlocking Us.

As the Leaves Fall
by Gillian Gabriel

As the leaves fall, so do I, down on my knees.
I grab handfuls of red, orange, yellow, amber,
Rust, ruby, gold. I throw them as high as I can,
Flutter my eyelids as they fall,
Fall down on me, rainbow confetti.

I smell their dampness, earthy and raw, cleansing and
fresh,
Peaty and homely. I breathe them in,
Until bittersweet too washes over me,
Dissolving my joyful grin.
How can I admire the beauty

When the leaves themselves are dying,
Falling to the end of a spring and summer that's gone?
My stomach grips and my head lowers,
Hands splay in dying leaves, tears plop off my chin.
Sorrow washes over this passing joy.

How can something so awe-inspiring
Draw in a cloud of heartbreak and longing,
An end to sunshine, hope, and thriving,
Replacing flip-flops with sturdy boots
And wiggly toes with woolly socks?

And then I remember, this tree
Is shedding her wondrous cloak to conserve, go inwards,
Then come back through tiny buds, joy to come again!
New leaves, new buds, pretty blossoms and fruits,
Yes, indeed, as the leaves fall, it's bitter and sweet.

Story behind
I Must Fall To Grow Again
by Debbie Moores

IN THIS POEM, I use the metaphor of the seasons, as seasons give me hope for the future. At the time I wrote this poem, I had just left a nine-year relationship. Living alone again, I felt lost, and struggled both emotionally and financially. This poem reflects my evolving acceptance that I had to let go of my nostalgia for what had been. I had to allow myself to feel my sadness – all of it – to heal and grow.

I Must Fall to Grow Again
by Debbie Moores

Clinging like an autumn leaf
Afraid to fall to ground
I miss the smell, the sights, the sounds
Of summer long gone now

I perch upon my fragile branch
Afraid that I must fall
I feel so tired, and withered
And still I crave the sun

I know the time has come
I must surrender. I must fall
So I can return to earth once more
And I can grow again

I'm hanging here now by a thread
Still dreaming of the sun
When days were so much warmer
But I do what must be done

Harsh Winter, I so fear you
But brave, I must be
For life and love to grow again
I must let go of the old me

I look down and it's so far to fall
But it's a journey I must take
So, I close my eyes and grit my teeth
Let go and down I fall...

Story behind
My Rose
by Humaira Naz

ROSES ARE ONE OF my favourite flowers – their scent, colours, layers, even their distinctive thorns. Their thorns can cause pain, and in this poem, they also feel pain.

I wrote this poem on the one-year passing of my dearly beloved father. Writing about him and talking openly about his passing were especially difficult for me when he first passed. A year later this poem emerged, and writing about him metaphorically, as a Rose, made writing about him gentler and easier.

When I was younger and could barely write, I would scribble words on paper, and my father would try his best to read them back to me. I think he would be proud of this poem.

Each time I visit my father now, I leave a rose for him, My Rose.

My Rose
by Humaira Naz

As petals fall,
No longer remain,
Even the thorns feel the pain

Of a loss so beautiful,
A loss so sweet,
Forever in the mind
A memory to keep.
Forever and now
Resting in peace.

Story behind
A Time to Honor
by Liora Rosen*

A VERY OLD AND close friendship that started in childhood and had many ups and downs over the years. The letting go took quite a while ~ a long time to fully acknowledge what was happening. It required being with what is instead of wishing it were different. This poem arrived at the moment I truly knew something had died. And there was no judgement, no argument. It simply was.

*Liora Rosen is a pseudonym

A Time to Honor
by Liora Rosen*

It feels like a death.
It is a death
of something,
of something that existed
that is no longer there—

an old friendship,
a very old friendship
that lost its rudder
and can't seem to move forward
anymore.

It feels like a natural death
a gradual slowing down
the heart beating
more slowly
more quietly,
the calm
after the storm,

after the endless trying
(it's this, it's that, it's you, it's me)
to make it work, to figure it out
to attempt to bring it back to life,
to what it once was

there's no such thing
as going back
there's only every other direction—
always new.

The old friendship is dying
it may have already died.

Will something new spring up in its place?
Always...

But now is the time ~
    to honor the death.

*Liora Rosen is a pseudonym

Story behind
Life and Death
by Aidan Lazzarotto

ONE DAY I AWOKE to the sounds of chirping birds dancing on the breeze outside my window. I lay in bed reflecting as the sun's rays streamed into my room. As I pondered there, my mind turned to the darkest of our earthly taboos: death. I noticed an odd misconception people have when speaking of death. Death has been denoted as life's opposite in nearly every discussion I have heard on the topic, either directly with words or in the framing of the conversation. While this may seem trivial, words and framing do matter. They define our basic assumptions about a topic. They set the groundwork for how we allow ourselves to look at, think about, and engage ideas. They change the way we ask questions, make decisions, and obtain certainty about the world.

Truthfully, I am not so certain any of us know what death really is.... Not yet at least. However, we are each destined to find out one day.

For that is our eternal contract: when we come into this world and take our first breath, a day will come when we must take our last. Drink deep of this earthly air, dear friends.

Enjoy it all.

Life and Death
by Aidan Lazzarotto

People talk of life and death
as though they are opposites.

But it isn't life and death,
it is birth and death,
the two bookends.

Life is all of it.

Story behind
Sometimes I forget, but mostly I remember
by Julie Foubister

THIS POEM REPRESENTS IN summary many lessons learned in my life so far. All lessons learned require a period of integration where we can expect to 'forget' on occasion.

A Cancer diagnosis has been the biggest catalyst for the unveiling and integration of everything I already knew to be true at a soul level. In order to survive we evolve and in that evolution we must experience death on many levels and ultimately we will all experience physical death. The underlying energy that animates can never be destroyed and when we begin to observe more frequently from this perspective we sit in the peaceful knowledge that there really is nothing to fear. In a lot of ways Cancer is actually what has saved me.

Sometimes I Forget, But Mostly I Remember
by Julie Foubister

Sometimes I forget.
Sometimes I fall into darkness.
Sometimes there is only fear.
Sometimes I become too attached to all that isn't now.
Sometimes I've felt like stepping off.
Sometimes in the past I've longed to go back to the place without breath.
Sometimes I feel that all that is, somehow isn't good enough.

But then I remember again.....

I remember that we only know light in contrast to darkness.
I remember that right now is all that exists and right now is so beautiful in its simplicity.
I remember I am alive. I remember to breathe.
I remember that I create my reality in this moment.
I remember that I always have choice.
I remember that whilst I am alive there is always hope.
I remember what I've always known to be true; that this life is heaven on earth.
I remember that a transitory glimpse turns into a lingering moment.
I remember that it is all perspective.
I remember that I am not the circumstances or traumas.
I remember that life unfolds in the direction I choose to look in.
I remember to choose wisely.
I remember that I am the observer.
And then,
I remember that nothing can hurt me from this place.

CHAPTER 4

FORGIVENESS

'Forgive the past and let it go with great gratitude. It will allow us to embrace the present and future with love, enthusiasm and passion.'

DEBASISH MRIDHA

Forgiveness is the ultimate in self-compassion. Finding a way to forgive strengthens us to move forward with intention and self-belief. It is not a weakness to forgive – it is a mature way to live in an imperfect world. It is to be truly vulnerable in a healing way. To put victimhood, persecution and perfectionism behind us, to welcome the beginnings of a new kind of self-esteem or self-respect. Forgiveness is nuanced and layered, and, in this section, we experience this courageous compassion in action.

Kate Jenkinson

Story behind
The Journey Saved Me *
by Ross Nichols

FROM THE END OF 2005, I experienced a slowly unfolding crisis of declining physical and mental wellbeing. With an ever-growing negative outlook, I found I could no longer do my job, and exited a career I had hitherto enjoyed. What I thought would be a six-month break before finding another job, turned into a three-year search for a way out of the black hole I found myself in.

At the time I had 2 young children who needed their dad, and a wife who needed her husband, so I was fully committed to getting well. I was willing to do whatever it took, and that commitment took me on a journey into previously unknown territory – my innermost self. I stumbled forward in the dark, and with the support of healers and guides, found a way to face my shadow and begin to love myself again. This poem tells the story of the greatest challenge I have ever faced, and how I overcame it.

* The Journey is a cutting-edge transformation and healing method pioneered by Brandon Bays. www.thejourney.com

The Journey Saved Me
by Ross Nichols

Consumed by guilt, grief, shame, and fear,
my body came to reflect
my inner world, pain, fatigue and misery.
If this was hell, I was in it,
my own peculiar purgatory.
I considered taking the easy way out
but couldn't do that to my family.

My spirit was crushed,
my light had gone out.
I had judged myself
and this was my punishment:
to be living on the outside
but dead on the inside,
a dead man walking.

My quest for redemption
led me to The Journey,
the courage to face my shadow,
make peace with it through forgiveness.
Now every day is my second chance.
I live, laugh and love again
and know I'm truly blessed.
The Journey saved me.

Story behind
My Shadow
by Kate Jenkinson

I WROTE THIS POEM quite a long time ago, after I had just left an organization. The organization had asked me to leave, as opposed to me deciding I was ready to move on. I was exploring what this meant for me and knew, as always, that when I was burnt out, I needed to go through some kind of recovery process. For me, poetry has always been that, so I went to a poetry workshop. I was trying to understand, as the poem says, the whole of me, of which my shadow is a part. At the same time, I also signed up for a Myers Briggs indicator licensing workshop to help ground me in learning and moving forward, rather than being bitter about the experience I had had.

In my explorations, I realized that my profile was, in a sense, the opposite of the western world profile – so it wasn't so surprising that some people in my company didn't "get" me. Upon reflection, I saw that, over time, I had adapted to their culture by leading from my shadow qualities, as opposed to from my heart. As I saw that, and tried to work out what to do next, I endeavored to embody my whole self in any new experience; to move into any new position from a deeper place of acceptance of the whole of me.

I did eventually find a more well-suited position with a corporate HR team. While walking round a garden centre in America with them, I saw a gargoyle, partially in bright sunshine, and partially in shadow. I saw it as a reconciliation, a homecoming, for myself – shadow and all. I took a photo of that gargoyle, and often share it with this poem.

My Shadow
by Kate Jenkinson

I want to know my shadow
its secrets to reveal
I want to love my shadow
no more to be concealed

If I can know the whole of me
of which my shadow's part
I know I'll feel a peaceful quiet
and a stillness in my heart

Story behind
Lucky One
by Frank Bolaji Irawo

I COACH LEADERS, AND MY COACHING yields great results. My clients' feedback is stellar. And yet, I doubted myself. There was misalignment between my self-perception and that of my clients. This is so common that it has a name, Imposter Syndrome.

With physical sight, what we see is made of two inputs: the sensory input of the eyes, and the meaning the mind attaches to that input. The latter is what dictates our responses, and hence our outcomes.

I use this poem with leaders who have moved up their career ladders but never feel deserving. Their own misalignment drives them to work harder just to justify their achievement, until in some cases, it leads to burn out. With this poem, I invite them to explore their perception in the face of contrary evidence.

In my case, I did a leadership audit. I realized I had been a leader for over 25 years. And I chose to align my perception with the positive feedback of my clients – even when I did not feel like it.

Lucky One
by Frank Bolaji Irawo

What am I doing here,
breathing in rarefied air,
operating above my station,
punching above my weight?
Can't help but feel I don't belong,
so grossly out of place.
Clearly, they could not find better.
I guess I had to do.

Purporting a picture of perfect grace,
belying my furious paddling beneath
barely holding my own to swans last seen
outside, in our man-made lake.
Must work harder to keep pace,
Maybe they won't notice
I'm out of place.
Might be just easier to fess up,
vacate my space.

A stroke of luck,
a fortunate alignment of events,
the question unasked is how long it would take
before they discover
I am an imposter,
showered with accolades I don't deserve?
If only they knew what I knew,
they most certainly would think the same.

If it looks like a duck,
if it quacks like a duck,
if it swims like a duck,
what are the chances it is a swan?

I worked, they saw.
I persevered, they trusted.
I delivered, they appreciated.
I stayed the course, they promoted.
Amazing how "lucky" I got,
the harder I worked.
A case of mass delusion?
An ever-repeating fluke?

What if I chose...
to suspend my disbelief,
to walk in their boots,
to see with their eyes,
to question openly,
to listen truthfully,
to open to the possibility
they like what they see?
If my work is good enough for them,
maybe it can be good enough for me.

Story behind
Fingerprint
by Gillian Walter

I WROTE THIS POEM after a client session. My client had been hard on herself, and critical about how she was showing up at home and for our session. She struggled to hide her flaws and mistakes behind a different, 'better' identity.

She spoke of her frustration with her child's fingerprints, which seemed to be everywhere in her home. The harder and faster she tried to wipe them away, the faster they seemed to reappear. We let that sit, but the metaphor of the fingerprint caught our attention.

We later looked at the beauty and uniqueness of a fingerprint; each one a mark that will never be repeated. I shared my observation that a fingerprint is like a labyrinth; each journey through a labyrinth too is unique, never to be travelled the same way again. I brought my client into written labyrinth work; we draw a labyrinth and write a problem inside it, moving in toward the center. Then we write all possible perspectives and solutions from the center back out.

After the exercise, my client was quiet, in a pregnant pause so conducive to insight. Then she said, "What if today were the last day I saw my child's fingerprints? What if I tried to preserve the last print she made?" There and then, she became determined to celebrate her daughter's unique marks and qualities, and to support and nurture her as she grew into who she was.

In the end, she saw the same in herself. She hugged her own inner child and committed to celebrating and nurturing her own unique and special qualities. She saw how much more powerful that was than trying to be someone else.

Fingerprint
by Gillian Walter

A fingerprint is a sign you were here,
Left in a place you hold so dear.
And even when wiped away,
Your identity mark is here to stay.

Not only on a surface, mirror or thing,
But in your echoes, dreams and played heartstrings.
A travel stamp in life's passport,
A unique pattern only you brought.

Celebrate the prints only you could leave!
Forgive, cry, laugh, learn and grieve.
Then paint your hands and print anew
The Brave Heart colours that reside in you.

Story behind
Mother
by Julia Heubeck

WHILE THE EXPERIENCES OF my childhood were real to me at the time, I was only freed from their shackles through understanding and forgiveness. Acceptance was the only way I was able to become who I was meant to be, and to live in rhythm with my purpose and flow.

Mother
by Julia Heubeck

Mother. Where are you?
You were always my illusion,
somewhere close,
never to be touched.
How, without love,
did you create
this pulsing heart?
Your absence led my path.
I travelled blindly,
knew the demons in the dark.
I felt their eyes upon me,
their noses sniffing
for traces of my love.

Starving beasts,
let loose to feast
upon my unspoiled flesh.

Who else but you
could shield and defend me?
Innocence lingered, a sweet deceiving scent.

Words of rancid pasts
spilled from the void
where I longed to find your heart.

In the absence of your touch
I was deprived of my senses.
Your eyes told stories of disgust.

I remained static, frozen in confusion,
Not knowing that to live or to die
were two separate choices.

How could I love
from a desert of affection?
How could I see divinity

when all I could remember
was pain, birthed
into a world of fear.

Mother, is forgiveness the answer?
Does your humanity
deserve my love?

As the seeds of truth
are watered by my tears,
your lessons wither.

To love you once more...
My path is clear.
I shift my longing

from my heart's fibrillation
to the rhythm of my soul,
an echo of the universe.

Chapter 4: FORGIVENESS

Story behind
Wheelchair Access
by Hélène Demetriades

GROWING UP I HAD a very difficult relationship with my father who was emotionally and physically abusive towards me. He was also a very secretive man, and I had felt shut out from his life. I grew up in Switzerland until I was nine. My father kept a separate flat in the city of Lausanne, an hour and a half journey from us, to which we were never invited. He even told my mother once that he didn't want her to visit the flat as it would bring him bad luck! He lived there during the week and would travel home to our village on weekends. Even when we moved back to the UK, he kept his flat and visited Lausanne regularly. I kept my distance from him in adulthood, but in the last three years of his life, I spent a good deal of time with him in his nursing home in the suburbs of Lausanne. It was during this period that we experienced a new-found intimacy, and to some extent, I got to know the town to which he had been so connected.

Wheelchair Access
by Hélène Demetriades

I longed to share the places
that drew you in your daily life
mapping out your spirograph of town,
intimate mandala of your *va-et-vient*.

Lausanne's newsagents, restaurants,
sleek shops and banks, that catered
for your necessities and the delicacies:
the *Herald Tribune*, smoked salmon,
Bally shoes, Lombard Odier.

I am grateful for these years,
your wheelchair has allowed me access.
We've sat on café terraces
soaking up the sun,
shopped for trousers
and a pair of dark green slip-ons.
Navigated pavement edges
breached old divides.

Story behind
Weep and Pray
by Dearbhaile Bradley

I KNOW JUST HOW EASY IT IS to fall into the illusion that no-one else understands how we are suffering. We believe we are alone in our pain. It was Stephen Levine in *Healing into Life and Death* who first introduced me to the idea that we can relate differently to our suffering, open up to it as a place where we connect with everyone else who is suffering. This helped me relate differently to the chronic pain I was experiencing, and enabled me to be more accepting of the limitations it set on what I could do. And this poem, which went through many stages, is the synthesis of my journey to connect and accept.

The line 'The heart that breaks can contain the world' is modified from a quotation* by Joanna Macy which I also found a powerful and helpful idea in coping with deep grief. We will all know times when difficult feelings arise, and acceptance can transform how we experience them.

*'The heart that breaks open can contain the whole universe.' is the original quote.

Weep and Pray
by Dearbhaile Bradley

Just for today weep and pray
and do not say it is 'useless', 'pathetic', 'stupid'.
Just for this moment let yourself stay
in touch with what is to be here, now,
alive, on this planet, hurting.
Just for today do not run away –
let tears slip along the grooves
worn by losses intimately known
and do not judge.

All griefs are one grief.
All tears are the ocean.

Open up. Permit. Let be.
Allow pain to swell the size of suffering all.
Let yourself weep even though
you cannot see the value in it.
"The heart that breaks can contain the world"
and today you feel humanity
crying in your heart, so weeping is your work.
So just for today let yourself weep and pray.

For today is a day when you know what it is
to watch your baby starve, slowly,
sad eyes grown huge, closing,
when you know what it is to realise
the little flutter is fluttering no more,
and no-one will ever know who they were.

Do not say you do not know,
that you have not been to such places.
The pain you know is the pain we all hold.
This knowing dwells in our hearts
for all we may seek to escape it.
So just for today, let yourself weep and pray.

You are blessed to have this time
to let your tears fall for us all.
You are blessed to be here now
even if all you can do is allow
yourself to reach out and touch
gently with your thoughts
all the pain that's held in the world.

The raped and tortured,
crippled and murdered
are reason enough that just for today,
you let yourself weep and pray.

And because you are where you are,
you can take it one step further:
to open your heart beyond those who are
easy to embrace in love, and honour in tears,
to the boys who drop the bombs,
as well as the people they drop them on,
to the business men who spend their working hours
designing instruments to torture
and those who find their use a pleasure.
The sadistic and cruel, the tormentors and killers
are family too, and so you include them.
Weep that they are the way they are,
pray that something might change them.

So now you've looked at the world the way it is,
let the whole world rest within your heart.
Honour your willingness to look at the truth
of the consequences of our choice not to look.
Return now to your grief's familiar grooves;
see how softly they sit within your heart's breaking
and forgive yourself.

Let every tear become a prayer
that hearts may heal everywhere.
Learn to see this 'being with'
is your offering, is your gift,
and it's okay that just for today
it is your turn to weep and pray.

Story behind
When Dreams Die
by Aidan Lazzarotto

I AM WHAT YOU CALL "A PLANNER". I make great plans, built upon vaulting ambitions and grand visions. In my work, this way of thinking allows me to help clients see new possibilities and forge new paths in life. This trait is part of my personality, yet it can also be considered a skill.

My capacity to envision the world as it could be... or rather, as it should be, helps me transcend the boundaries that insecurity would otherwise place on my imagination. It allows me to stick to my goals and find creative paths to reaching them. It gives me great staying power, for I am clear on my desires and able to recalibrate when I am knocked off course. This capacity has helped me move through the most difficult moments of my life by offering hope and inspiration.

And, it has far too often been the source of my torment.

Let me put it this way.... Have you ever tried chasing the horizon? It never gets any closer, does it? It is beautiful to look out at the sky and see what the horizon has in store, for after all, the horizon is where sunsets occur. However, we must remember that life isn't happening *someday*; it is happening right here, right now, in *this* moment.

When we live from the present, we may find happiness is not something we must chase. Rather, it has found its way to us of its own free will.

And what did we do? We let go.

When Dreams Die
by Aidan Lazzarotto

Sometimes your dreams have to die
so that you can live.

Step into what is next.
See what you become.

Story behind
Unforgiveable?
by Frank Bolaji Irawo

FORGIVENESS WAS A THEME that came to the fore when my father passed away several years ago. Every time I spoke about him after he passed, I had a sense of loss over what could have been – if only he had shown up and met my expectations of what a father should be.

I subsequently came across the declaration below, used by Dr Wayne Dwyer to release the negative emotions he had about his father.

"From this moment on, as I send you love, I send you kindness. Who am I to judge you? Who am I to condemn you? Who am I to be critical of you? I don't even know what you were living through and why you had to do what you did. I send you love from now on."

This helped me come to terms with the fact that my father did the best he could with what he had, and with what he knew. I realized that to forgive and release was not to condone what was done. Instead, it was the greatest gift I could give myself. Holding on to the hurt only prolonged my suffering, and prevented me from experiencing a richer life. I had been allowing the past to rob me of a better future.

Hurt and pain can become our constant companions. We can even become addicted to that pain, and then unwittingly attract yet more pain into our relationships and our lives.

I use this poem to help my clients consider who is paying the true costs of unforgiveness, and to help them break that cycle. Now is as good a time as any.

Unforgivable?
by Frank Bolaji Irawo

Can't believe you would even suggest it...
to forgive and validate the evil done
to forgive and betray my memories of loss
to forgive and deny the gravity of my hurt
to forgive and release them from their guilty sentence
let go the story of the wrong they have wrought.

It may very well seem unforgivable.
The question on the table though –
Can I afford not to?
It's not them, but me, this poison is harming.

Can I forgive and be unshackled
from the sentence of these memories?
Can I forgive and let my healing begin?
Can I forgive and take responsibility?
I can.
I start my journey into the light,
a gift to me, only I can give.

CHAPTER 5

RESILIENCE

"In the midst of winter, I found there was, within me, an invincible summer."

ALBERT CAMUS

Most speak of resilience as something we cultivate, build and learn. Perhaps in some practical ways we do. Yet, when we look at nature, we see resilience everywhere. We see trees grow from a speck of dirt on a rock face. We see flowers pop their stalks through pavement. We see laughter and love erupt in lives engulfed in poverty, loss and war.

When we look at our own lives, have we not, each of us, survived every experience to this day? Sure, we may feel a bit scratched up. Sure, we may feel weary, tirelessly tested. Sure, we may have tapped every tool in our toolbox, and even begged some from others.

Yet all the while, whether we noticed it at the time or not, and through our starkest winters, our "invincible summer" remained invincible, enduring and immutable. When we pay attention, we can see that resilience is our very nature. It is the essence of *all* nature, and the essence that brought us here, to this page. We celebrate this together, in poems and stories of our innate and remarkable resilience.

Sharon Strimling

Story behind
Breath Finds Us
by Sharon Strimling

I WAS DEEP INTO my healing journey before I realized that that which was "healing" had never been broken. I'd been diagnosed with PTSD, anxiety and depression, and had never questioned that I had years of work to do before I could live as a well person. But in a moment of inquiry, I took that to task.

I looked back on all the moments in which I had forgotten myself – helping a friend, falling into laughter or even grief – and saw that in fact, in every one of those moments, I was *all there, nothing missing.* Nothing I had been through had broken my capacity for life. It was, and I was, already fully human: rich in each moment with joy or challenge, connection or aloneness, inspiring thoughts or terrifying ones.

At one time, I had discounted momentary presence as distraction. But as I looked closer, it was more than that. It was aliveness... exactly that which I had been seeking.

When clients and I look together, they too see this for themselves. Their need for a better experience softens, they fall more easily into now, and paradoxically, in the end, they fall into their wellbeing.

These moments, this breath, find us. And when it does, we touch the living wisdom baked into our presence. We realize we are the intelligence of life itself, and we can breathe.

Breath Finds Us is an ode to the remarkable presence that shows us we are already home.

Breath Finds Us
by Sharon Strimling

Let me imagine my words could
make your day one breath lighter.

Let me imagine they could wrap you in clouds,
bathe your feet in a warm sea,

guide your knitted brows back,
find space behind your searching.

Let me imagine they could knit their obsidian
shapes
into cashmere, caress your wind-burnt cheeks.

If my words could do that, I'd write all day.
For I've too known lost. I knew lost a minute ago,

an hour ago, a lifetime ago.
And I've known home – as you have

in the breath between stars and puddles,
in the breath between ~ life spins space.

Space for me, space for you.
Have you noticed?

Or have you been searching,
chasing breath like butterflies?

Shhh.... Breath will find you.
In the red and gold of New England leaves,

in new life and new death,
in losing ourselves in compassion,

in the taste of chocolate,
and the slide of velvet,

breath finds us. In moments
swept into love, or laughter,

or even, yes, in the swift river of grief,
breath finds us. She finds us.

So let the search behind your eyes
rest, and your lost be found.

Story behind
Next Step
by Julia Heubeck

IN MY TEENAGE YEARS, when I didn't know what to do, I experienced a kind of paralysis, fraught with intense fear and pain. My path was never clear to me, and in my confusion and turmoil, I followed the path I believed society and culture dictated.

Over the years I have learned that when I don't know my path, I can pause; I can trust that I will eventually know the next steps that will be right for me. I learned patience, and that sometimes doing nothing is the key. I learned to trust to wait until my "next step" appears, and rather than knowing the goal today, I trust what is right beneath my feet.

Next Step
by Julia Heubeck

Forever I've been needing
To do the next best thing
To fuel my greed
To stomp out fear
To feel that I am here

And then one winter morning
I did no longer know
The next step seemed impossible
I felt my worry grow

For I had just done everything
The world had asked of me
I waited and decided
That patience is the key

I felt relaxed
My mind switched off
My soul had time to breathe
It was so very simple
Needed no mastery

There is an inner wisdom
Which knows it all along
Attuning to what is inside
Will lead where I belong

Story behind
Being Me
by Elisabeth Goodman

WALKING IN NATURE IS one of my go-to strategies for mindfulness and wellbeing. As I walk, I gradually free myself from restless thoughts, and tune into all my senses. I wrote this and other poems, a series entitled "Wellbeing Musings", in the final year of my mother's life and read them to her in her final hours. She loved nature and practised meditation. I like to think that she heard my words and that hearing them brought her joy and peace.

Being Me
by Elisabeth Goodman

Being held by the trees
as I walk between their pale trunks
and glowing greenery
is not just about tuning into Nature.

It's also about tuning into Me.

There's the physicality
of my feet treading the hardened paths,
the breeze blowing warm and cool on my arms,
the silence between the cars.

And there's that core at the centre of me;
the will,
and the joy,

of being me.

Story behind
Tree
by Anna Springett

THERE IS A HUGE LARCH TREE at the back of the house where I live, it fills most of the view from my bedroom window. It is the kind of tree that sways and moves with mesmerising movement. When I sit on my bed, thinking and reflecting, worrying or planning, my eyes inevitably go to the tree: I cannot help but wonder whether all my moments are caught up in her branches. She is like a constant companion to my highs and lows; she's been there for me throughout the past few years. I have written a few poems where she features – such is her presence in my life. Sometimes, it is as though she expresses my thoughts and emotions more powerfully and subtly than I ever could.

Tree
by Anna Springett

That tree is my everything
Has captured my life in its boughs
Split down the middle as two trunks
of independent strength
How shallow are its roots, how deep
It fills my vision
Shares my past
Holds the air and wind that whips and wastes and wanders
Stays the same and changes all the time
Cut into portions that mix and meld
Across the artificial boundaries of my seeing
And still stands –
Toing and froing
Coming and going
Ebbing and flowing
She stands – knowing, not knowing

Story behind
I Think of My Grandmother
by Cara Wheatley-McGrain

I WROTE THIS POEM on International Women's Day 2022, inspired by my many coaching conversations with clients – particularly female clients – in the post-pandemic space. The pandemic sparked a period called 'the great resignation', and as work and domestic spaces blurred, we explored their choices.

Our zoom calls throbbed with a powerful and thrilling sense of possibility, as many people questioned the career trajectory they had previously felt they 'should' follow. They, and this poem, speak to resilience, and the importance of looking to the past to make sense of our present – particularly at times of rapid and unexpected change.

This is a poem inspired by my very real, Irish granny. She was both soft and strong. Her very presence embodied quiet dignity and great resilience.

I Think of My Grandmother
by Cara Wheatley-McGrain

Born in 1909, into a world where
she could not vote, where no woman
held public office.
She was a nurse, a mother of six.
A strong and dainty woman
who loved navy
and wore white lace collars.

I think of my grandmother,
her soft skin and blue eyes.
The quiet prayer she whispered,
as she sprinkled holy water
on my sister and me,
swaddled in pink.

I think of her busy hands,
baking bread, pouring tea, folding
clean gingham tea towels and,
on special occasions,
holding a rare cigarette,
poised and daring
between bright red lips.

I think of how she would walk
for miles, barefoot
on the long Clonea strand,
clutching her shoes, skirt gathered up,
so she could feel the cold Irish sea
between her toes.

I think of my grandmother,
the joy on her face,
her ready laugh,
her knowing steady smile,
and her four daughters,
all soft and strong at once,
who cycled and travelled widely,
and strode into the world knowing
they could work, and vote, and speak.

I think of my grandmother today.
Her memory held
in my black and white photo, soft focused,
eyes staring bold and bright.

And I think of my grandmother's grandmother,
who lived through famine and loss.
How her grace and her strength
held her family firm.
Her hands that baked and formed
and moved through soil and sea
to feed her children.

I think of her today,
my grandmother's grandmother,
not caught in a photo frame,
but held in my memory,
in my blood, in my bone.
The shape of her lip,
the curve of her cheek,
her fierce strength to exist, persist,
in the face of impossible odds.

And today I am grateful
to all the women
who have gone before.

Story behind
Shrines
by Jennie Linthorst

SOMETIMES LITTLE 'SHRINES' CLING to us as much as we do to them. Breaking free from their old energy can require a fresh burst of resilience. We push forward into new terrain, while not leaving our cherished memories of loved ones behind. This tricky balance plays out in Shrines.

Shrines
by Jennie Linthorst

I unpack last boxes of files for my new office,
purge bent thumb tacks from a donated bulletin board,
sense a stir in my heart for change.

My hand lands on a black frame with gold edges—
my mother's young face, a ghost stuck in time,
smiling in her ivory pearls and cashmere sweater.

Her gold hoop earrings catch the light.
A woman about to slide into her dying,
before cancer's final victory 38 years ago.

It became a ritual to rehang this photo in every new space—
dorm room, apartment, bedroom, office.
Now I question this shrine

moved from place to place,
question this relentless need for her frozen presence
in a life I have lived without her.

I want a different memory on these fresh yellow walls.
On my next trip home, I will search albums in my father's closet,
to find a photo of me in my mother's arms.

I need what I can no longer remember—
the feel of her arms around me, her smell, her voice.
Nurturing, I will never receive trapped behind glass.

Story behind
Mourning
by Lori Michael

THIS IS ONE OF a series of poems I wrote around the time of my mother's passing, when I had just turned 33. As the older child in a single parent family, I was super close with my mother. Part of me truly felt that if she died, I would die, too.

As I sat with her during her time of passing, this being the first time I had experienced being with someone who was transitioning, her passing seemed to me more like a birth than a death.

I remember distinctly that on the day after her death, I was able to clearly discern, in a way that I never had before, the life force that was keeping me alive despite my feelings. It was as if it were distinct and separate from me. It had an energy and a will of its own. I was being lived.

That force had its own beauty, like sunlight, and was not personal. In its light, there could be no such thing as survivor guilt. Hence the lines, "you will walk gently, tentatively, out on the day, / bathed in the same bright light / that carried her away."

"Mourning" pays homage to that ever-present life force.

Mourning
by Lori Michael

There will come a morning
when the one who brought you into the world
has left it
empty of those welcoming wings
that ushered you in and
hovered,
protecting,
until you knew no world without
those wings.

There will come a morning.
You will curl yourself into a ball and
bury yourself in night,
as if you could
follow.

Then,
foiled,
you will walk gently, tentatively, out on the day,
bathed in the same bright light
that carried her away.

The whole world
belongs
to such a morning.

Story behind
Loss
by M Bukowska

I AM NO STRANGER TO PAIN, loss, and grief. Yet, when my friends suddenly and unexpectedly lost their child to an undiagnosed condition I was all too familiar with, there were just no words that could bring even a semblance of a respite.

As I sat with my own grief, and my guilt for still living, and tried to remember how I moved forward in times of great pain and sadness, the poem came to me. I shared it with my friends and it brought them some hope for solace.

At their request, and in tribute to their resilience, I included it in my book, "BrokenHearted Wisdom".

Loss
by M Bukowska

When you suffer a terrible loss
that shatters your entire being,
and you wish you were dead
instead of going through
the nightmare,
remember that there will be one moment
when you wake up,
and notice that life sucks a little bit less,
that your heart beats a little bit easier,
that breathing doesn't hurt as much
And in that moment you realise
that maybe not tomorrow, but one day soon,
you'll be OK again
And until that day comes,
you'll survive

Story behind
Anxiety and Me
by Ross Nichols

IN 2018, I DISCOVERED I had the ability to write poetry when inspiration struck. I later wondered if I could write poetry by choice. This led me to experiment – to use the act of writing a poem to explore something on my mind. This poem, *Anxiety and Me*, is the result of that exploration. I found it hard to begin; however, the rhythm and metre for the poem emerged as I wrote. I worked on the poem over the course of a week, and wrote more verses, some of which I discarded. This final version feels a fair reflection of how I experience anxiety, and how I'd like that to be different.

Anxiety and Me
by Ross Nichols

I look at the clock, my mind boots up,
No drowsy lie in here.
Tension grips my stomach, my mind beings to churn.
Anxiety has its way with me.

We're auld acquaintance, Anxiety, and me,
I've known you all my life.
Yet I've only recently recognised you.
How I've paid the price.

Welcome to my world my friend,
All calculations and dread.
I'd love to sleep the whole night through,
Wake without you in my head.

I'm coping very well with you,
through avoidance and control,
but it only takes one extra task
and I'm in overload.

Deadlines hang over me,
My biggest source of stress.
Until I've finished all my work
I really cannot rest.

Don't talk to me about resilience,
I get the whole idea.
You try to see things as they are
When your mind is full of fear.

How will my story end?
Is this how I'll always be?
I'd like to find a way
To live more peacefully.

I gather it's not uncommon
For humans to be this way,
What is it that so drives us?
What holds us in its sway?

Maybe it's because we're human
With all our complexities.
What lies beneath our surface?
What is our history?

As I get to know you better,
I think that you should know,
You've been my companion long enough;
It's time for you to go.

Will you e're come back again
and rob me of my ease? No.
It's time to let you go my friend
and live my life in peace.

Story behind
I Want to be Well
by Ross Nichols

THE EXPERIENCE OF WRITING a poem by choice (see *Anxiety and Me*) proved to be insightful for me. I decided to repeat the exercise and explore the topic of wellness. I'd trained as a Wellness Coach and discovered that I found it easier to describe illness than wellness. Writing this poem helped me to articulate what wellness means to me, and the different perspectives people have, and that just because we are not ill does not mean we are well.

I Want to be Well
by Ross Nichols

When someone says, 'I want to be well',
Do we reach for a pill or call the GP?
Do we assume they are ill and want to be fixed?
Or do we take the time to listen?

What is wellness? What is illness?
Are they universal?
Is wellness the absence of dis-ease?
The clue is in its name.

When we are out of balance,
In our being, must be a reckoning.
Like double entry bookkeeping:
Cause in one place, symptom another.

To restore wellness, should we treat
The symptoms or the cause?
Do we look backwards, or look forwards?
Do we follow a trail of tears? Or instead, a trail of dreams?

Do we need someone to fix us,
Or can we find our way?
Do we want to be well?
Or does our dis-ease somehow serve?

It's not straightforward, wellness.
Illness, easier to grasp.
We can always ask a doctor to treat us.
But will that make us well again?

Story behind
Fear
by Julia Heubeck

SO MANY YEARS I spent in anger and resentment; fearful of judgment, shame, not being good enough. I fought the people closest to me, but also innocent bystanders; spent my energy on people who didn't care, and who wouldn't fight back.

My fighting and fear left me exhausted and frustrated. Once I realized that fear is useful to tell me where to look, but deceitful in its instruction for action, I was able take a different stance.

Now I stand up for myself and what I believe to be right, but I have learned do this with grace, leading with kindness and acceptance rather than aggression.

Fear
by Julia Heubeck

I have fought in countless battles
Wrapped in armor made of fear
Built with ingenious precision
Never let a crack appear

With a shield of tears for defense
And a horse of rage for pace
I led the charge in fury
Let confusion win the race

Fear has led to little glory
For countless battles I have lost
My enemies refused to fight me
Indifferent to my army's costs

Today I have a sword of courage
Sanded by will, polished by grace
I cut free of my armor
Ready now to lead the brave

Story behind
The Dare
by Sarah Moores

CERTAIN EVENTS CHALLENGE US to be courageous. That's when we discover we are more resilient than we thought, as we know we could bomb, yet we do them anyway!

International Coaching Week was my annual 'Dare I?' challenge. Every year, I'd sign up, excited about what I'd share, and start preparing an experience and a speech.

Last year, however, I tore up my prepared speech the day before. I had realised that I would be more in tune with my audience if I spoke directly from the inspiration in my heart following the experience we'd all shared.

This year, as the universe conspired to require complete spontaneity, I wrote 'Dare I', and delivered both the speech and the experience with only a moment's preparation.

On reflection, I recognised that what I hadn't taken time for was panic. I simply hadn't given myself time to worry, over-think and project fear into my task. In the end, I realised how little time was needed to achieve some things, and how much time and energy we can waste stressing about them.

Tell yourself you can, and you will!

The Dare
by Sarah Moores

I used to worry whether
I did or didn't
Should or shouldn't
Had or hadn't
Could or couldn't

Until the time came when
I couldn't, but could have
Can't, but would have
Shan't, but should have!

Because opportunities come and go
When we don't say yes, we're saying no
The moments we don't seize, we're letting go
To receive a catch, we must dare to throw

So throw yourself, catch my eye
As time catches up, there's no catch if you try
Time for yourself, time for I
Before time catches up, it's time to try

Do it for yourself, do it for I
Do talk yourself up, do TRY
Dare yourself, dare I?
Before the dare's up, let's dare to try!

Story behind
Promise
by Dearbhaile Bradley

SOME YEARS AGO, I worked with two other poets, Rachael Clyne and Jo Waterworth. We called ourselves 'Strange Sisters'. We created performance pieces by weaving our poems together. One of our favourite exercises was to find a line in prose or poetry, and then each write a poem containing that line. The seed for this poem was 'Every beginning is a promise.'

The recognition that our past does not determine our future is central to the way I work as a coach. Separating our identity from what we habitually do, think and feel is key to being able to make the changes we want to make. I love the simplicity of this poem as a way of getting that significant point across.

Promise
by Dearbhaile Bradley

You can always begin again.
Wipe the slate clean.
Turn over a new leaf.
Draw a line under life.

Release the past.
Forget history.
Let it all go.
What do we know?

Place your counter on the first square.
Blow on your dice, toss them in the air.
Let their fall dictate how you will play.

All the people you have ever been
have no say in who you become;
not unless you want them to –
not unless you let them.

So
you are
free
to be
whoever
you want
to be.

Every beginning is a promise.

Story behind
Advice to 12-year-old me
by Kate Jenkinson

SOMETIMES PEOPLE DON'T SEE the best in us, and sometimes we don't see the best in ourselves. Sometimes the things we've been asked to tone down are our best assets – our hidden or underground resources. As a child, I was often asked not to laugh in the classroom. However, fun energised me and helped me get through the parts of my lessons that bored me. I realise it must have been disruptive for my teachers, but by being quiet and toning down my enthusiasm, I lost interest, and more importantly, lost a part of me.

Now, as a coach my enthusiasm is something people value. Making learning fun engages my clients, and knowing when to laugh, and how to enjoy work and life, is a powerful source of resilience.

Maybe you can write a letter to your 12-year-old self, letting them know what was right about them all along?

We can all be our own worst critic at times, so why not give yourself credit for who you always have been? Why not love your strengths?

This poem was originally shared as a writing prompt in a wellbeing workshop to help people appreciate more about themselves, and to help end the stigma of poor mental health.

Advice to 12-year-old Me
by Kate Jenkinson

You know what Kate?
You got it right!
You loved your friends,
enjoyed your life!

Don't fret or feel
you are misplaced
or missing out.
You nurture an underground
fountain of joy for the human spirit.

You ride
an ever-flowing river of fun,
a readiness to live,
a fulfilling future for yourself,
your family,
any who choose to follow.

Don't let the melancholy
in your soul speak
louder than your dreams.
That yearning, though hurting, is turning
you into a wellspring
of hope and optimism.

You see all the silver linings.
When others shiver, damp in mist,
your stubbornness resists.

Your vision is defining what's possible.
Your light is glowing.
And I, now knowing,
in a world of uncertainty,
your future is safe with me.

Story behind
The Greatest Courage
by Susana Rinderle

THIS POEM CAME TO ME early in the COVID-19 pandemic. It's about letting go, trusting, knowing our proper place on the planet, and re-orienting ourselves – as individuals, cultures, and *Homo sapiens* – towards the subtle wisdom of the heart. We are capable of astounding accomplishments, but can also be grossly immature in how we make meaning or insist on certain outcomes.

Our planet has a larger intelligence, and we're embedded in multiple complex systems. We're not the masters of our destiny, and this might be a good thing. Learning to listen, discern, trust, and give up the falsehoods we've been told about how life works might be the start of a better life for each one of us.

The Greatest Courage
by Susana Rinderle

There exists no greater courage than this:
To love
with no guarantee of requitement
To trust
with no guarantee of safety
To strive
with no guarantee of success
To believe
with no guarantee of satisfaction.

There exists no greater valor than this:
To create
with no hope of immortality
To speak
with no hope of listeners
To stand
with no hope of change
To live
with no hope of survival.

We can scale murderous peaks
vanquish impossible Goliaths
in a hostile arena
run fast as a gazelle
with steel blades for feet
migrate whole civilizations
and rebuild entire cities from the scourge
of plague or maelstrom.

Yet there exists no greater courage than this:
to allow the heart
to be our ever-changing compass
faith our engine
and divine Wisdom
its fuel.

Story behind
Sparring
by Sharon Stirmling

Alex (Moon) was 16. She spent four days with me at the request of her frightened parents. I liked her right away. She was an impassioned actor with a theater scholarship and a quick wit. Our first morning, Alex described the relentless spinning of her mind and how her only relief came from cutting. She searched my face for the worry she had come to expect. I paused.

Cutting is interesting. The violence of it frightens us. Yet, behind the pathology lies an essential and healthy drive – a drive for a quiet mind. Pain will momentarily accomplish that, cutting through rumination. So will alcohol, exercise, food, sex.

I wasn't afraid. I knew Alex was simply in need of three things. One, she needed to understand that she wasn't trying to hurt her body, she was trying to save her mind – an innate intelligence misdirected. Two, she needed to understand the true nature of thought as imagination in motion. Three, she needed to understand that she was not — and had never been — her thoughts.

We looked together at the harmlessness of thought, even when terrifying, dark or stormy. We looked at how thought is creative, life giving, sometimes wild, and always transient – a river that keeps flowing when we let it, a thunderstorm that passes.

I asked Alex if she'd like to hear my crazy thoughts. What ensued was a "Sparring" game. She needed me to win, and I did.

Realizing the underlying intelligence that drives our actions, and discovering the benign nature of thought changed my life at Alex's age. PTSD, anxiety, and depression cleared. When I realized I was not my thoughts, my world changed. Now Alex's had. I check in with her from time to time. Her anxious thoughts come and go. I smile and say "mine too." Relieved, she goes back to rehearsal and gets on with life.

Sparring
by Sharon Strimling

"Oh that's nothing," I said,
sparring with her
for the most terrible thought,
the most unforgivable,
the most ugly, and insane.

Moon sat across from me,
seventeen, ocean eyes wide,
jaw slack, stunned soft,
steeped in every shameless
word.
"That's nothing," I said again.

Moon sparred back.
She wanted to lose, of course.
Which was good.
I wanted to win.
I set the match to see

her scarlet thoughts wither
in the dark shadows of my own,
so vile and so innocent,
imaginal, harmless
and human.

I wanted her thoughts
to pale -
dried and dusty roses,
ever beautiful,
and never hers

to crumble, to fall
gentle
back to the soil
to the mystery
from-whence-they-came.

I wanted her thoughts to fade –
monster shadows
on moonlit walls,
so terrifying, then gone
with the sun.

Moon and I,
we wanted her to lose,
and she did.

"That's nothing," she said,
her thoughts illumined,
seen for what they were,
seen for what they *never* were –
her.

Moon and I,
we wanted her to lose, as she did,
so that she too, beautiful Moon,
could one day spar with another girl
suffering the illusion
of madness.

Chapter 5: RESILIENCE

Story behind
Pearl
by Gillian Walter

WE WERE ON A FAMILY HOLIDAY in the same seaside location in which a friend of ours grew up. As it happened, she was there at the same time, as she had lost her mother and was getting her affairs in order.

Our friend was very generous with her time and showed us beautiful sights, and then took us to a visitor's centre that specialized in pearls, where a knowledgeable attendant taught us all about them. We learned that oysters can either make shell or pearl around each irritation they encounter. That struck me as a powerful reminder of my own choices. As we walked around the pearl centre my eye was drawn to a single, black Tahitian pearl.

My friend caught me gazing at it and asked if I'd like to try it on. I replied, "Absolutely not." I told her there was no way that I could afford something so impractical for myself when there were so many other 'important' demands on our family wallet. She then shared with me one of her mother's favourite sayings as she was growing up: "Know your worth, girl!" She asked me if I knew mine.

I bought the pearl and have worn it every day since, as a vivid reminder of the choices I make, and of my own unique worth.

Pearl
by Gillian Walter

The pearl within you
Born of struggle
Layered with challenge
Polished by wisdom and
Rainbow coloured
Yearns to be worn
Longs to reflect
New iridescent light
On survival gifts

The pearl within you
Protects a heart
Uniquely yours
It rises to the test and
Lovingly gifts
Tough shell or pearl
The choice remains
Your pearls reflect

Wear your pearl with pride!
Sing of life's gifts
Adventure gems
Wear your worth
With courage and joy
Welcome new skin
As enamel shines
Welcome your pearl
To sing!

Story behind
Empowering Choices
by Sarah Moores

THIS POEM IS PART OF MY LOCKDOWN JOURNEY.

I treated the enforced retreat as a self-growth journey. During this journey, a professional musician friend who had long wanted to produce something close to his heart, transformed my perspective-challenging poetry into songs. Songs grew into an album, then further evolved into a moving meditative experience to free the body and empower the mind.

This Empowering Choices poem was born from the recognition that we often make dis-empowering choices through either fear of the unknown, or fear of judgement.

As a Journey Practitioner*, I offer a 'Conscious Choices Process' which allows us to wake up to what it feels like to continue a trajectory we know isn't for our highest and best. It's an uncomfortable journey that gives us just enough leverage to step out of our comfort zone, and into our miracle zone. Harnessing the power of the sub-conscious, we over-come self-limiting beliefs to embody our own strengths, empowering us to take the required leap of faith. We experience what it's like to walk our own path, to our own drum. We open our eyes to what we really want to do, why and for whom.

It's life changing to follow the call of one's own heart.

Following my own heart's call to record my voice, trusting that it would be what others needed to hear, and performing live, took people on a transformational journey of my own intuitive making. It required me to overcome limiting beliefs, self-judgements and feelings of fear and inadequacy. It's been fulfilling to witness my fears turning to excitement, as I sense a greater purpose behind what is still unfolding.

* The Journey is a cutting-edge transformation and healing method pioneered by Brandon Bays. www.thejourney.com

Empowering Choices
by Sarah Moores

This path, that path,
  Which shall I take?
    This way, that way,
Fear I'll make a mistake...

Forwards, backwards
  This way, or that?
    This road, or that road?
Need to choose the right track

Marching, running,
  But in circles, I fear.
    Headless, groundless
My vision's not clear

    I take a breath to regroup
   Take a pause to reflect
  My purpose won't be to get there
Without love, or respect!

    So take a moment to find balance
   Take a second to recharge
  No prizes for stressing
No true purpose is harsh

    Remember your path's your own,
   Your choices to make
  Your freedom lies before you
When THIS responsibility, you take

This path, that path
Doesn't matter which one.
This way, that way?
Take your pick, just have fun!

Your path will come clear
You will KNOW what to do
As your heart is PULLED to it
That my friend, is your clue.
Trust your choices,
As trust empowers you!

Story behind
Catching the Sun
by Aidan Lazzarotto

HAVE YOU EVER NOTICED the rhythm of your life's journey? Have you viewed your life as scenes from a movie? Or as music? Perhaps if you listen deeply enough, you will hear a soundtrack.

We strive valiantly to be heroes within our own story, yet heroism can be both comedic and tragic. The tragic hero gets caught as an unchanging person in a changing world and suffers greatly. Their unseen parts corrode the foundation of their future.

What then separates comedy from tragedy? What allows us to pull seed from shell and enjoy the nourishment within? What allows us to laugh at our misfortunes and pursue peace of mind?

Within our lives is a hidden order that we uncover through a gentle gaze. Its cardinal sign is an engulfing peace of mind, a sensate senselessness, a state of flow. It is a state we can experience regardless of the circumstances around us, while not invalidating our experiences of misfortune.

Bad things happen to good people, to be sure. Yet it is not what happens to us that marks us for tragedy. It is not the events of our lives that make us a tragic hero, or a pawn in another's story. It is what we do with the life we are handed; it is the attitude we choose and the actions we take.

And here is the trick we were never told as children: the actions we take are a direct response to how we see the world. Thus, it is our perceptions—or our willingness to notice and challenge those perceptions—that determines the quality of our life.

At the end of the day, your life comes down to how you make sense of insanity.

Catching the Sun
by Aidan Lazzarotto

Life is a funny thing,
given and taken,
so easily lost,
buried within us,
yet not far away.

We seek it in spaces
where we used to play,
catacombs waiting
full of dust and decay,
within our minds.

And yet while we're seeking,
we hear the chimes
of knowledge and wisdom
and poetic rhymes
calling our name.

But over the mountains,
we were promised fame.
We judge when we stumble
and call ourselves names.
We hide from our failures
and highlight our shames.
We give in to fear.

Though when we settle
our minds become clear,
we hasten our progress
and let love draw near,
we put down our struggles,
and choose to stand here,
catching the sun.

Story behind
Instructions
by Susana Rinderle

AS A PROFESSIONAL COACH and trauma-informed resilience practitioner, I see too many bright, talented, caring professionals and leaders buying into the inhumane beliefs of our modern workplaces. Beliefs that we need to work harder, do more with less, and grow despite the limits of natural laws that are not only oppressive, but killing us.

Driven by fear, we may collude with abusive expectations in toxic organizations within extractive industries, then wonder why we're individually or collectively miserable, unhealthy, or violent. But we are also very powerful beings.

This poem reminds us that those beliefs are lies, that those ways don't work, and that, in our power, we can choose differently.

We are but one *very* recent species on an ancient, wise planet. Our sanity and joy amidst chaos is enough to catalyze deep change.

Instructions
by Susana Rinderle

The world requires not
your clamor and clang
your doing more of the same
striving and fighting
trying to move boulders
that will not move.
Pointed fingers and pointed words
anguish and anxiety
belie your belief
that they are more powerful
that they are winning.

Winning does not matter.
Winning is doing.
It's a worn out space
inside a crumbling frame
hung on a rotting wall.
You may lose.
You will die.
Humans go the way
of the trilobites.

There is nothing more radical
than sanity amidst madness,
nothing more subversive
than joy amongst misery,
love inside violence.

Find yours.

Do not despair
nor languish in resentful apathy.
Let your anger and integrity
stoke the engine fires of your belly,
lighting the jewel of your heart,
igniting the force field
that is You.

Open your bright eyes.
Let those ancient frames
sigh into dust
and fall from the walls.
Lock the door behind you;
Tomorrow
will be too late.

Story behind
Hope Restored
by Elizabeth Papalia

TOO OFTEN I SEE people living under a persistent sadness. I see it in my family. I see it in my community. I see it in parts of my own heart. It can be easy to slip into an acceptance that eternally aching hearts are normal, and that happy days are distant and dreamlike.

The truth is, with deliberate self-awareness, support, and a space to talk, we can transform our futures beyond our wildest dreams. Hope is real. Restoration is real. And the motivation to take action lies with us. It is we who can pursue restoration. It is we who move past our past, and step with hope into a transformed future.

Hope Restored
by Elizabeth Papalia:

Keenly aware of sadness and sorrow,
of long-time tears falling from past pain.
Acutely conscious of hearts hurting,
Faces weeping, red-eyed, and flushed.

Struggling to verbalise the root
Of weaknesses long-buried, avoided.
Soft, fearful tears trickle
Emitting sorrowful whispers.

Haunting shadows of struggles,
Grown bigger over years.
Depression let out, in sight of a few,
A few who most always knew.

Aching hearts wish for happy days,
Days that seem dreamlike and distant,
Futures that could be true if renewed
With action taken for healing.

Make the cycle of bruised,
soul-damaging decisions stop.
Shift perspective, confront and talk
Through wounds and scars, still red.

We can all build a new frame, from pieces of old,
Life chosen to hold our tomorrows.
So our refreshed, restored hearts can step out,
Forwards. Forwards towards hope.

Story behind
Riding the Waves
by Olivia D'Silva

I USED TO STRIVE for those days where everything fell into place and made sense. I would use these days as a measure of how well I was doing in life. And when life didn't make sense, I would strive to create sense of it, which was often a cause of angst.

But what was I doing there? I was discarding those down days and moments of confusing uncertainty. I didn't like these days because I didn't like how they made me feel. I would judge these days as a reflection of how badly I was doing in life.

Riding the Waves began as an expression of these two 'sides' of life, these opposing experiences. What emerged was an expression of wholeness, and the resilience to welcome each day.

Dark brings context to the light. We only know the light because of the dark.

Throughout my seven-year coaching career, I have continued to work with my own coach. I dedicate this poem to her as the one who supported me on my own personal journey of learning to ride the waves. Thank you, Teresa.

Riding the Waves
by Olivia D'Silva

The day will surely come
When disparate threads of your life
Finally merge into one
Your sacrifices make sense
Unfinished stories find their place

Storms of confusion gently calm
You put your feet up
Turn your face to the sun
A soothing breeze of meaning
Flows through your troubled soul

And you pronounce this day 'Perfect'

Then, instead of enjoying it
This perfect day
You try to grasp it, hold it
And in that gut-wrenching moment
Your perfect day goes

The day you worked so hard for
Hoped for, for so long
Swallowed up by the familiar
Fearful unknown
Your ever-open questions

Do I belong?
What do people think of me?
What will become of me?

Will I ever be happy?
Or am I destined to trudge through life
Begrudgingly?

But of whom do you ask these questions?

What kind of answers do you need?
Because holding this moment
Is like bottling the sun

A glimmering illusion that can never prevent
A torpid nightfall
Gloomy doom
Disillusioned despair
Solitary confinement
Or "Nobody cares!"

Deepest dark days, bad days
Hold-you-down days
Days you thought you'd dealt with, left behind
Follow you like quicksand
Swallow you from nowhere

But rather than holding, or discarding them
You learn to ride their waves
The freedom of the highs
The constraints of the lows
The exquisite mundane moments in between
All that weave life's rich tapestry

Then you turn a new blank page
Continue this story in your own precious, unique way
Where each day is perfect, in its own right
And you rest in the light

Because you've known the hard-won treasures
Of the dark night

You hold your head high now
And march through every season
On the momentum
Of this glorious unfolding life

CHAPTER 6

LIFE

"Each time a door closes, the rest of the world opens up."

PARKER J. PALMER

Life is the kaleidoscope between the two profound mysteries of birth and death. As you journey through the poems in this final chapter, may you discover new hues and reconnect with familiar shades, reflecting the myriad colours of your own life, both those that have been seen and those that are yet to be revealed.

Tracey McEachran

Story behind
Curiosity by
Kate Jenkinson

AS A POET AND a scientist, I've always been acutely aware that there are many ways to look at things. That has intrigued me. I'm always curious to understand people and their perspectives.

In my work as a leader, curiosity plays a powerful role. It stops me short of judging differences as problems. It allows me the joy of experiencing new, original, or unique perspectives, strengths and talents.

If we understood work more deeply as a human endeavour, one that brings out the unique attributes of each person, then we might have more curiosity around our mistakes, resistance and poor performance. It would certainly be more fun to work with each other!

Curiosity is a powerful and inclusive attribute. I encourage everyone to develop more of it.

What does it mean to be curious? As I ask myself that question, I find both answers and more questions!

Curiosity
by Kate Jenkinson

What is your favourite word
and why?

I ask with curiosity,
as that's my favourite word
you see.
It speaks with generosity
for the human spirit,
our ability to be similar
and yet different
every minute
             of the day.

And with curiosity
you can never say
I don't have time for that
right now. No,
with curiosity,
you make the time
to really understand each other.

Curiosity is not just a verb.
It's a noun; a thing.
A curiosity is something
original and unusual
and worthy of understanding.

Now, with our generosity of time
and our curiosity of spirit
if we made time to understand
each other in work,
we'd have much more fun
being in it!!

Story behind
Empathy
by Nathan Blair

WE COULD HAVE CHATTED for hours. Gosh, we were having a blast! Alas, the time had come for us to say goodbye. The front door closed behind them, and I was alone once more. I bathed in the silence.

Out of this silence emerged the muffled melody of my neighbours talking.

I thought this an excellent metaphor for the empathic attunement required within a coaching conversation. A core competency for coaching, and most helping professions, is the ability to sense and respond to our clients' inner worlds. We learn to notice, with increasing accuracy, the constellation of signals that reveal our clients' beliefs – beliefs they may hold about themselves or the world around them.

From our inner silence and attunement, we notice a change in emotional tone, a spontaneous gesture, a subtle shift in facial expression that makes the implicit explicit. We learn to track those signals and bring nuanced listening to our clients that opens doors to insight and self-awareness.

It is easy to share observations or work skilfully when clients' signals are overt, calling out for attention. But when signals are quiet, or barely perceptible, we need our own quiet to hear. However, internal monologues can clutter up our presence. Questions like "Where are we going with this?", "Am I doing a good job here?" and "What should I say now?" arise.

We learn to notice the noise, and then let it fall away. We rediscover our even deeper silence. From there, our clients can be heard. Their whole bodies speak to ours. And from there, they hear their own bodies speak.

To be heard beyond our words – now *that* is a marvellous thing.

Empathy
by Nathan Blair

We don't tend to hear
What's going on inside
Our neighbour's home

Until
It's very noisy in theirs
Or very quiet in our own

Story behind
The Whisper
by Todd Roache

THIS POEM CAPTURES A moment of being called within to discover 'beyond myself'. That is, beyond the parts of my inner map that have already been charted, and into the blank space where the known 'me' ends and mystery and discovery begins.

Re-reading this poem, I realize the sensitivity it took to hear this call, the curiosity and courage it took for me to follow it, and the humility it took to remain in discovery and not-knowing. I recognize the presence and love I needed to nurture my call's revelation and blossoming, and the commitment it took to give this process its due time and attention.

I am fascinated by, and grateful for how many shades, nuances, corners and layers exist within us – beyond those we already know.

Endless treasure awaits...

The Whisper
by Todd Roache

"Come inside,"
whispers something within me.
"Tread gently

with pure intention,
pristine presence.
Be open to beholding
beyond yourself.

There are petals here,
aching to open
and receive your wonder.

There are dew drops sparkling
in the light of your soul,
each a world of their own.

There are colours with no name
that will sigh in relief
as they see themselves
in the flame of your witnessing.

Aspects yearning to unfurl
under the sun of your exquisite attention,
and be carried into the world
through the sparkle of your new-found eyes."

Story behind
Enough
by Sharon Strimling

SOME DAYS I THINK contentment is life's greatest healer. It points us to the truth of this moment, unique and precious, no matter what it holds. Contentment lands us firmly in our lives as they exist, free from an illusory future moment that will never come.

Sometimes it is all we can do to hang on – to make it to tomorrow. Sometimes just breathing is enough. Other days, tomorrow can't come soon enough. Life brings it all.

I don't always feel like I'm enough, that I have enough, or that life is enough. "Enough" is a grace that just comes, with no credit to myself – a gift I accept with gratitude.

Enough
by Sharon Strimling

I sit here content.
Not gushing. Not
grieving. Not feeling
inspired to change
the world. Is that
the stuff of poetry?

It should be. Like I
made it to this
couch, warm and
here, and that's enough.

Story behind
Grief
by Rona Rowe

MY FRIEND DIED EARLY in the pandemic. She was in America, far from me in the UK. I had met her nearly half a century ago at university. I was an undergrad, she was a PhD student, twenty years my senior. We were both interested in beauty, as an idea and an experience, and how to be fully autonomous women in the world. She witnessed my young adulthood with generosity and joy, and shared her family with me when mine was far away. She enriched my thinking and my life. I feel her loss still.

Grief
by Rona Rowe

Grief is a wordless truth
a quiet push and pull
beneath the everyday waves
of loving and living,

Quiet, until a deathly pause
exposes the howling echo
that travels forever
backward and forward in time,
susurrations of white water
on a seashore,

I stand face to face
with the
relentless eternal.

Story behind
Soul Circle
by Dearbhaile Bradley

I WROTE THIS POEM when a group of people I loved and had been working with over a period of years was falling apart. It was so painful! I needed to find a way to express my belief that when we are willing to be open and trust the process, any conflict becomes resolvable.

It always seems ironic to me that such a hopeful poem arose from a place of deep pain and despair. It is an affirmation of the fact that change is always possible. No matter how bleak this moment is, healing exists. With a willingness to be truthful, listen with an open heart and keep going, we find peace and resolution.

Soul Circle
by Dearbhaile Bradley

My heart aches for a soul circle
where we humans form the hub
and in the centre, Divine Spirit
guides us all in love.
A circle of equals
united in interest,
celebrating the diversity
we find within our midst,
knowing our strength is in our differences,
our willingness to hold conflicting perspectives.

But all there is, is us'uns
with our faults and failures and foibles,
and all the bits left over
from our imperfect childhoods –
anger and pain, fear and impotence
endless battles of our little egos,
our incompetent communications,
and inability to handle conflict.

So how's it going to work then?
this transition to the future
when each of us embodies
the woundings of our culture?

We fumble our way forward.

Keep speaking truth.

Keep listening.

Keep going

until we find that place of healing,
evolve into a soul circle
where we humans form the hub
and in the centre, Divine Spirit
guides us all in love.

Story behind
The Abundance of May
by Jen Blaxall

HAVING A DEEP CONNECTION WITH NATURE, I offer guided walks and nature therapy in the New Forest. May is a time of new beginnings, hope and abundance. As an energy healer, May is also the time of year I get out of the therapy room and into nature to heal myself and others. Out in nature, in May, my clients and I are filled with hope, light, warmth, abundance and love.

The Abundance of May
by Jen Blaxall

Bluebells and cuckoos come to mind
when thinking of May, leaving darkness behind.
Trees are lime green as they come into leaf,
while cubs venture out, cutting their teeth.

Swallows and swifts swoop and dive,
as the natural landscape comes alive.
Nests of birds are starting to fledge,
and bracken unfurls along woodland's edge.

Cow parsley verges and flowering meadows,
colour and scent step out of their shadows.
Dragonflies rattle in purposeful flight,
and skylarks sing from impossible heights.

Bats forage as day turns to dusk,
and birds chorus on their early dawn busk.
Mayflower hedges are busy and alive,
with pollinators and butterflies who productively thrive.

As the crab apple blooms on this glorious Beltane,
my wishes for you and nature's the same –
new beginnings, light, warmth and prosperity,
in utter abundance with love and sincerity.

Story behind
We Are All This
by Cara Wheatley-McGrain

THIS POEM WAS INSPIRED by a coaching supervision retreat on the British Jurassic Coast, where coaching mixed naturally with sunrise sea swimming, forest bathing and walking across ancient fossils on the ammonite pavement.

This retreat enabled us, a group of coaches, to bravely explore the edges of our practice. It challenged each of us to cross thresholds and to extend our coaching conversations into a liminal space where deep transformation is possible.

The heart of *We Are All This* was written whilst seated in silence in a sunlit forest glade, drinking harvested nettle tea.

We Are All This
by Cara Wheatley-McGrain

Nose deep in water, its push and pull suspends me
I am rain returning to ocean, river, stream
The endless movement of water, vast and gray
Touches the earth and air at my sides
The slow motion of mist across the sky
the steam of atoms returning to air
I am the shape of water

The sound of air pushed between wings
The cry of the lone gull
I am the bright spirals of ammonites caught in rock
Ancient, and layered
The writer letting go of each old narrative
Pen pushed to page

I am the bright light of the beetle-wing
Sunlit cobwebs, filaments of motion, ivy round your trunk
The gentle sycamore, earthed by soil
The fearless leaf released from its branch
Soft lime moss lit from within
The tiny motion of chlorophyll in each vein
The atoms of light caught in a raindrop

We are all this
Nature – Breath – Motion
Air in delicate alveoli
Oxygen softly slipping through stomata
The tendrils of mycelium
Holding the tips of roots and loam
The hand of the writer
Letting go again and again.

Story behind
from the heron i learn presence
by Lori Michael

MY SON AND I are blessed to live on five acres surrounded by woods and water. A river flows by our property and we can watch the sun and moon reflected in a large pond just behind our windows each morning and evening as they rise. Better still, we are surrounded by wildlife: deer, hawks, rabbits, squirrels, snakes, so many lovely birds...for a season or two, a family of foxes... not long ago during a time when the waters were high, an otter who came to stay in the pond while his river home was inaccessible and who entertained us with his rolling and splashing...and quite regularly, a heron who hunts for fish in the mornings in the pond just outside my bedroom window.

I often spend part of each morning listening to guided meditations that take me deeper into what is known as the perennial nondual understanding. On the morning I wrote this poem, I had been listening to a meditation by Francis Lucille. His words, "we are always home," resonated deeply. Later, during what turned out to be a busy day, I found myself stopping by the window to watch the heron. Her movements, and her stillness, came together with the perfume of Francis' meditation in the form of this poem.

from the heron i learn presence
by Lori Michael

from the heron i learn presence,
the presence that disguises itself as patience.

so still for so long, watching the water,
seemingly more at peace in the hunting

than in the apparently less peaceful
diving for, catching, and wriggly swallowing

of the fish, the heron unlocks for me the quiet triumph
of savoring the journey as attentively as one savors the destination.

after watching her for a while, i move more slowly,
stopping to see and take in the lovely sights of the suds on the dishes,

the quality of sunlight in morning stillness,
the here now and fleeting face of my son.

"we are all, always, already home,"
said in stillness, said in standing,

with awkward elegance, perfectly imperfect grace,
spoken in the quiet language
herons know and teach.

with thanks to francis lucille

Story behind
An Alembic on the Threshold
by Hélène Demetriades

THE WAY IN WHICH MY FATHER DIED was his greatest gift to me. I spent the last five days of his life by his bedside. I was fortunate that it was my turn to visit him. Apart from carers coming in and out at various times, I was alone with him, holding vigil. It was a challenging five days. He had a fever and was in and out of consciousness. I witnessed him 'decoupling from his body'. He only spoke twice, once to tell me I was hopeless, and once, to cry out for my help. On his last afternoon he was resting after having been given an extra dose of morphine. We were undisturbed for those last few hours. It came to me to sing the mantra from the Buddhist Heart Sutra: 'Gate, gate, paragate, parasamgate, bodhi swaha!' 'Gone, gone, gone beyond, gone utterly beyond, what an awakening! Amen'. On my mac, I found a version of the mantra sung by the singer Deva Premal – I switched the recording on to back up my own singing. The poem is about what happened next.

An Alembic on the Threshold
by Hélène Demetriades

I sing as your body shuts down,
watch the doors of your mind
fly off their hinges
a white sun pulsing through your eyes,
your chest an alembic
gathering you with each breath you suck in,
I witness your birth as you die
as you suck in your last breath elated,
finally fully alive
and you don't expire, but keep hold
of the breath and take wing
as I gaze into your brilliant face on the bed
not knowing you've left, mesmerised.

Story behind
The Tsunami of Transition
by Gillian Gabriel

THE TSUNAMI OF TRANSITION was inspired by an image of the sea. The image reflected for me the ebb and flow of my authentic self as it has been revealed over time. Like waves that never stop moving and changing, and that take on different shapes, volumes of power, and at times I can feel in flow with it or I can be swimming against the tides, and sometimes I'm sucked down by undercurrents. It's about my voyage of resistance and letting go to find my voice and to speak that to be me.

I now see myself becoming the wave rather than being drowned out or overwhelmed by it. Neither under it or on top of it, but it. Always changing, evolving, emerging, in transition from moment to moment, day to day, week to week, month to month, season to season, year to year, life stage to life stage, life to death, death to my soul's next calling.

Tsunami of Transition
by Gillian Gabriel

How do I surf this tsunami of transition
So it doesn't submerge and drown me out?
I swim, frantic, against the tide,
Physically, emotionally, spiritually
From my inside out.

I feel you swell and at times I'm drowning,
Pulled under by your sheer force
And all you want from me, for me.
How do I let go, flow
Subside with you,

Feel you wash over me instead?
Then under, as you support me
With compassion and care,
Holding me gently, as your choppy currents
Turn to ripples instead.

Relief,
Floating,
I flip my tail out of the water,
Dive headfirst into the depths,
Cold, clear, crisp, beautiful.

A calmness returns
Breath in my lungs
I move my body in time with you
Swirling all around
And through the storm.

I emerge from the depths.
My head and shoulders bob
Above the waterline.
My face turns towards Mumma Moon,
Stars aligned once more.

Story behind
Watch Me Roar
by Gillian Gabriel

WATCH ME ROAR IS ABOUT NOT KNOWING who I was and finding myself shard by shard over the years. It's about being told I should be quiet, hidden, and know my place. It's about taking on the identity expected of me, influenced by gender inequality and homophobia.

And it's about upturning these beliefs that held me down, and realising that if anyone knows who I am and what I'm about, I do. It's about saying enough is enough and choosing to stand up for who I am and what I believe in. It's about accepting all parts of my story, and choosing something different for myself.

Watch Me Roar
by Gillian Gabriel

Where has my voice gone, the belief, the strength
Now just a squeak, the plea of a mouse
Mostly ignored, not heard, not listened to
Shhhh "less noise!" bellowed from above

Don't make a sound, be still, be quiet
Tip-toeing around, scared to wake the giant
Holding it all inside, filling up the bucket
Squeezing more in, careful not to spill it

But the liquid is churning, swirling and swashing
Bubbles stirring up from the bottom, they're popping
Too much to say, no order or reason
A rising voice finding its season

Autumn to **release** all that's been suppressed
Winter to **explore** what to say for the best
Spring the time to **create** the story to be told
And Summer to **express** all that's been withheld

Then watch me roar towards the sky
No more tears, doubts, fears, "who am I?"

Story behind
GLEE!
by Todd Roache

I REMEMBER FEELING UTTERLY gleeful at the end of a day-long client retreat. I wanted to share that feeling with the world. I wanted to dance down the streets of the internet, as it were. (I live in the country with no populated streets to run down.) I wanted to shout my joy from the rooftops!

And yet, I found myself holding back, as if to share and declare my joy might somehow be rubbing people's noses in it. Then I thought about how I feel when I witness someone else with a big, free, radiant smile. It makes me smile too!

This poem recounts my evolution from noticing holding back, to letting my feelings flow, to sharing my joy with the world – unrestrained – as I added my last exclamation mark.

When we dare to share, it gives others permission to show up fully too. How marvellous. And for me, that makes any vulnerability experienced in sharing well worth it.

GLEE!
by Todd Roache

Is it ok to say
Hooray?

Why am I even asking...
when I could be basking?!

Not in glory
about 'my amazing story',
but in simple glee!

Innocent joy bursts
almost unexpectedly, then
checks itself to see....

Is it stepping on toes?
Should it go back inside
and hide with my woes?
No... I don't think so.

So here it is –
GLEE! For a great day
that blew me away!

And for the simple fact
I get to do
what I do.

Wahooooooooooo!
Yippeeeeeeee!

GLEE!

Story behind
Prayer to the Divine
by Julia Heubeck

ALL WE ARE LOOKING for is already within. The irony is we search outside, instead of inside, for our divinity. I wrote this poem during a retreat, during a moment I felt whole; a moment I allowed myself to be guided from within and completely trust in what was to come. I felt immense gratitude for my humanness in that moment, being allowed to experience all there is. This poem reflects that moment.

Prayer to the Divine
by Julia Heubeck

I am Divine and fully human
Who else can birth what's innocent
Who else can roar like a lion
Who else can squash it in its hand?

Who else can touch our souls with
laughter
Who else can cry our tears of joy
Who else can sing our songs of silence
Who else can drown in tears of wrath?

Who else is timeless and fully present
Whose else's silence breaks a heart
Who else can trust in their own madness
Who else can walk the path of love?

For I am fully, fully human,
And I am fully the Divine.
I am the prayer
And the compass is my heart.

Story behind
Honouring Simplicity
by Anjli Gheewala

I WAS INSPIRED TO write this poem to help people make rewarding choices about decluttering and organising their space. I have helped many people get organised, especially in their homes. Our energy, motivation, and emotions are influenced by our surroundings, so it's important to create our spaces in a way that supports us.

Poems have distilled wisdom, they capture essential truths. This poem came to me at a time when I was connected to both the challenge and the satisfaction of releasing and rearranging. I hope it will support anyone who wants to simplify their space in a meaningful way.

Honouring Simplicity
by Anjli Gheewala

There is confusion,
when we have too much.
All the thoughts…
How to keep? How to store?
How to sort? Where's the space?
We need this, we need that.
Nothing is enough. Or…
it's all too much.

We crave balance, but
we need stuff.
We want simplicity, but
how to get there?
Overwhelm!
Know it too well.

What does it mean 'to have'
if having brings stress?
Do we need things that
crowd our peace,
clutter our minds,
drain our time,
steal our energy?

Do we own things,
or do things own us?
Attachments, memories, history.
Desire, longing, joy.
Held in materials
we keep revolving.

Contrast.

We come with nothing.
We leave with nothing.

In truth, our things do matter.
They enhance our lives
in nameless ways.
A privilege of our era.
So then, sort with wisdom.
Discern.

Let go of what holds you back.
Keep what lifts you up.
Release what brings you down.
Set yourself up to feel good.

Breathe.
Rejuvenate.
Redefine what counts.

Make new decisions
for true desires.
Be symbolic and intentional.
Initiate the environment
that supports your
harmony and evolution.

This is courageous work,
emotions at play.
Simplifying means
new choices,
difficult choices.

Don't rush,
And don't wait.
Freedom awaits on the other side.

Now, what will you do
with your freedom?

Imagine.

Story behind
Beliefs
by Kate Jenkinson

I WROTE THIS POEM in my early forties, just after I had experienced an acrimonious end to one of my corporate roles. I was unhappy and searching for answers, questioning what I had done wrong and what I could do differently.

It was then, through coaching, that I learnt about limiting beliefs. I saw the belief I had been carrying that I was "not as important as other people". This belief had led to me putting others' views above my own, and to feeling overwhelmed, angry and rejected. I realised I couldn't change my past, but I could re-evaluate my beliefs for a different future.

At that point, I was able to accept that 'I was at least as important as everyone else'. I still had some more personal development to go to reach the empowering belief I have today: 'I am at the centre of my life'!

Beliefs
by Kate Jenkinson

Your beliefs lie gently
between your potential
and your reality

Are your beliefs
a delicate silver filigree
through which your hopes
and aspirations pass?

or, has Autumnal fall
perpetuated
and your beliefs lie heavily
        on your dreams

knee-deep
    rustling
        dry and dead
as you kick your way through life instead?

Afterword

THIS BOOK ENCOURAGES READERS to experience personal transformation, empowerment and healing through insightful poetry and personal stories. It suggests 10 ways in which poetry can be used to support coaching, and how there is synergy between a poem and the story behind it.

If you would like to be part of the Poetry for Coaching Community, please stay up to date with Poetry for Coaching, by following our accounts on:
Facebook https://www.facebook.com/poetryforcoaching
Instagram https://www.instagram.com/poetryforcoaching

If you'd like to interact with other fans/members/readers and authors join the Poetry for Coaching Community group on Facebook
https://www.facebook.com/groups/poetryforcoachingcommunity

There may be further volumes of *Poetry for Coaching* in due course. If you would like to register your interest as a coach poet, or be informed when further volumes are published, please contact the Editor, Ross Nichols, at: info@transitiontransformers.co.uk

Directory of Poets

The Creative Coaching Collective / Co-editors

Anjli Gheewala

See p. 61, 79, 297

www.anjligheewala.com

https://www.linkedin.com/in/anjligheewala

https://www.instagram.com/anjligheewala

Anjli is a writer, designer, organiser and coach who loves to work with creativity and colour. Currently in the Marketing field, her first career was in textile design. The creativity and methodical approach of that experience remains with her. Layout, style, and space are at the heart of her craft, whether working with content or home organising. Harmony comes both visually and functionally, and the diverse threads of her experience infuse both into her work. When coaching Anjli works with mindset-awareness. Clients and colleagues feel calm in her presence and deeply heard. She brings creativity and practicality to her pursuits in home, work and business.

She loves working with words, art, colour, visual story, and being a part of creative collaborative projects. She is truly grateful for the opportunity to use her skills in service of this book, which brings poets together worldwide.

Dr Kate Jenkinson

See p. 165, 181, 185, 241, 267, 301

Kate@nextstephr.co.uk

www.nextstephr.co.uk

Kate is a research Biologist turned award winning HR leader and now Executive Coach. With over 25 years' corporate experience in Engineering, Education and Life Sciences across UK, Europe and India, Kate is a trusted, credible partner to a leader's development. She helps global clients shift limiting beliefs, refocus coping strategies, shape development goals and take purposeful action. Kate creates the safe spaces needed for self-expression and exploration, enabling deep transformational insight and empowering personal and professional progression.

Kate is a Business Poet and sought-after Spoken Word Artist, incorporating her love of words into her business. Identifying as Neurodivergent, Kate employs creative practices to guide the development of other Neurodivergent professionals. Kate believes in the power of poetry to humanise work; epitomised by this Poetry for Coaching publication. Kate co-hosts open mics for performers with hidden disabilities, uplifting marginalised voices, providing platforms for people to be heard and to shine.

Tracey McEachran

See p. 17, 19, 21, 25, 99, 265

Tracey@curiousmindsconsulting.com

Tracey McEachran is a team and executive coach as well as a multi-media artist working with large format photography, film, sound, and installations. Her creative practice sits within the genre of portraiture and still life, employing constructed sets and existing backdrops to reveal contradictions in the human experience. Her work explores myths and the ever-present tension between group and individual identity. After working for 20 years as a senior leader in a large corporation, in 2007 Tracey left to pursue her ambition to achieve a degree in the arts. After gaining her BA in contemporary photography in 2010, she went on to graduate with an MA in fine art photography in 2012. Since then, she has been working as a professional artist alongside her career as a coach and facilitator. She predominantly works in the social housing sector on all aspects of culture, leadership, performance, creative thinking, and well-being.

Sarah Moores
See p. 107, 123, 237, 251
www.emotionalalchemy.earth
www.sarahmoores.co.uk
mail@sarahmoores.co.uk

As an Emotional Alchemist, Sarah helps us strip away our emotional lead to reveal our worthiness within. So often the greatest distance between us and our goals is the emotional baggage undermining our confidence! Harnessing the power of the subconscious and superconscious, Sarah is a Journey Practitioner, coach, mind-body therapist and Qigong teacher.

Writing poetry gives Sarah insight into what's arising within her psyche. Her head clears as negative thoughts are creatively expressed, enabling her to witness, rather than stay attached to her feelings as they pass through the prose. As her believed story transitions, higher consciousness flows in with a new perspective.

Creating transformational movement meditations to music from her perspective-challenging poetry, Sarah believes her emotional alchemy M.A.G.I.C. formula to be key because we can be lifted out of the limited cerebral belief that who we are is not enough, into experiencing ourselves as infinite beings of possibility.

Ross Nichols
See p. 7, 9, 115, 117, 183, 229, 233
info@transitiontransformers.co.uk
www.transitiontransformers.co.uk
Linkedin: Ross Nichols – Salisbury, England

Ross is the Editor of Poetry for Coaching. He served 26 years in the British Army. The experience of reading great poems and stories shared on social media by other coaches inspired him to collect them as a resource for the profession. He mentors and coaches business owners, directors, and professionals for: business; leadership; career; wellness; and cancer. He mentors other coaches for professional credentials with the International Coaching Federation (ICF). As a supportive member of the ICF, Ross is part of the team writing the Body of Knowledge for the coaching profession. His coaching style is Transpersonal, working with values, energy, vitality, and spirit. He is drawn to working with the shadow side, which is where he believes the learning and healing is to be found. Ross leads the Creative Coaching Collective, the Salisbury Coaching Circle and the Cancer Coaching Community.

Elizabeth Papalia
See p. 13, 41, 261
elizabeth.papalia@growintolife.com
www.growintolife.com
www.linkedin.com/in/elizabeth-papalia

Elizabeth, a warm-hearted, creative Wellbeing Life Coach, after spotting Ross's outreach, was glad to support this project. Having written poetry since childhood to express emotions, thoughts and experiences, knowing that the therapeutic benefits of poetry would be highlighted through this work was fantastic.

Since leaving f/t teaching, she runs Grow Into Life and helps people towards reshaping their busy, overwhelming lifestyle to include sustainable wellbeing habits. Building community is a priority everywhere she lives. Alongside her husband, she is beginning to renovate their beautiful, old townhouse in France and developing a creative wellbeing retreat. Find her YouTube channels @growintolife and @passionforpoetryandprose to learn more.

For years, Elizabeth has also supported the vulnerable and marginalised, working to offer safe and non-judgemental, mental health and ND informed spaces. In 2022, with Sean

Bennett, she co-launched a project called Coaching Through Crises, to connect people in crises with professionals offering pro-bono support - volunteers welcome to apply.

Sharon Strimling
See p. 91, 151, 207, 209, 245, 273
sharon@sharonstrimling.com
www.sharonstrimling.com
https://www.linkedin.com/in/sharon-strimling/

Sharon Strimling is a coach, speaker and writer who lives on a quiet island in a beautiful corner of the world. Smitten by nature and mystery, she writes to them, fumbles through them, falls into them. She tells of tall grasses and pounding waves, the noise of the mind and the quiet of the heart.

Having healed herself from PTSD in her twenties and inspired daily by her clients' remarkable mental health journeys, Sharon writes with authority to the brilliance beneath our shadows that can never be broken, that knows how to heal.

Sharon coaches youth, entrepreneurs, leadership teams, couples and trauma survivors. She offers retreats on Martha's Vineyard and internationally, and focuses her voluntary efforts on youth mental health.

Sharon jumped at the opportunity to help create this book, to bring the power of its stories to you. She is the final editor of all stories and poetry.

Poets

Uphie Abdurrahman
See p. 129, 139
uphiedragon@gmail.com
Facebook: Uphie Abdurrahman

Uphie is a mental health awareness speaker living in Jakarta, Indonesia. Uphie has volunteered in suicide prevention, awareness on childhood abuse and trauma, and normalization of neurodiverse expressions. Living with symptoms of and in therapy for ADHD, CPTSD, and quiet BPD, Uphie regularly speaks in public and private forums for mental health to raise more awareness about the issue. He writes songs and poems recounting things that happen inside his head, while aspiring to attain formal trainings on counselling.

Patricia Ahern
See p. 113
https://www.linkedin.com/in/patricia-ahern-7209561aa/
https://www.instagram.com/pacoaching_foryou/
https://www.tiktok.com/@patriciapoetry

I love creativity, curiosity, and imagination.

With positive emotional intelligence I have learnt that the essence of a happy fulfilled life is, growing into self-love and self-compassion, which I build on daily with mindfulness, meditation, positive affirmations and creative writing.

I love my inner child who reminds me how wonderful life is and my wise elder self who spurs me on to manifesting my dream future. I use writing wholeheartedly to tell my story of positive transformation, inspiring messages of hope and possibility.

I love my new path of ease and flow, more in control of emotional responses.

Helen Amery

See p. 57

hello@wildfigsolutions.co.uk

www.wildfigsolutions.co.uk

https://www.instagram.com/wildfigsolutions/

Helen loves helping people come into alignment with who they're here to be, while knowing who they really are.

She began her awakening and enlightening journey in 2018 after a turning point when she saw her development till then wasn't the whole picture.

After a significant awakening experience that year, she dived deep into the nondual direct path, alongside enlightenment of conditioned patterns that were keeping her out of alignment.

She now supports others in their own awakening – to know who they really are. And their enlightenment – to come into alignment with who they're here to be.

Nathan Blair

See p. 269

www.thesomaticschool.com

www.facebook.com/thesomaticschool/

www.linkedin.com/in/nathanjblair

As a child I felt the emotions of others deeply, so much so that I planned to get "EMPATHY" tattooed on my arm. I later came to believe that my sensitivity, which I'd thought was a weakness, could actually be my greatest strength. As a coach, non-verbal communication with my clients always felt important to me and I wanted to become more skilled in leveraging its power. The field of somatics encompassed everything I felt was fascinating about what makes us human. The Somatic School was born out of a desire to create the coach training I'd been searching for.

Jen Blaxall

See p. 43, 45, 281

newforestnatureandnurture@gmail.com

www.newforestnatureandnurture.com

www.facebook.com/newforestnatureandnurture

My name is Jen Blaxall and I live and run a small business in the New Forest called New Forest Nature and Nurture. I have a huge passion for nature and wildlife and have deep gratitude that I can share my love with others by offering guided walks and nature therapy. I am also an energy healer and enjoy helping people and animals through healing, holding circle and workshops. In my spare time I enjoy creative writing and recently published a children's book with my husband and regularly write wildlife blogs about my wanderings in the forest.

Sian Boissevain

See p. 55

sianboissevain@gmail.com

Facebook: ShannaMandira

Sian is an Artist, Poet and DJ.

Sian has, due to a troubled family history, delved in deep through years of counselling, and meditating, until finally finding The Journey, completing the Practitioner training program.

Sian also works as an Artist for Arts Care helping people express themselves through creativity.

She has completed certificate courses in Counselling with Art and Counselling, Rieki 1, Laughter Yoga and as an Osho Meditation facilitator.

Sian also started Pure Joy Conscious Dance parties bringing people together through Biodanza.

"These are all the things that make my day and I hope my poetry will make yours".

Dearbhaile Bradley

See p. 143, 155, 199, 239, 277

www.waystobewell.com

dearbhailebradley@protonmail.com

Dearbhaile is a mental wellbeing coach with over thirty years' experience of supporting people with mental health issues. She is also one of the Elder Bards of Glastonbury. In this capacity, she performs poetry at festivals and community events, and teaches creative writing.

'I see creativity and healing as flipsides of the same coin. It was in running a support group for abuse survivors, I first encountered the power of poetry to heal. I did not set out to write poetry. Rather, it evolved out of journaling as reflective practice when I was doing my Masters in Counselling.'

M. Bukowska

See p. 71, 105, 111, 227

Instagram/FB/Telegram: mb_magical_being

mb.magicalbeing@yahoo.com

M. Bukowska is an intuitive coach/mentor, a trained nurse, and a therapist. A gentle, intuitive, soulful being, who started writing poetry as a child to help her process the worlds around, and within, she authored "BrokenHearted Wisdom" (2019), "WholeHearted Wisdom" (2020), and "WholeHearted Wisdom – Poetic Journal" (2020), by Positive Energy Publications. She has immense empathy for all stages of grief, and emotions within all types of relationships. Her words will not only evoke a few tears, they'll reach right within, touching your heart and soul.

Colin Cafferty

See p. 127

https://colincafferty.com

colincafferty@hotmail.com

www.linkedin.com/in/colincafferty/

Colin Cafferty is an emotional intelligence coach based in Berlin, Germany. His noble goal is to nurture emotional well-being in others so that they flourish in service of a fairer society and a healthier planet. He writes poetry for himself, primarily as a means to process emotion.

Hélène Demetriades

See p. 89, 197, 287

www.helenedemetriadepoetry.co.uk

Twitter handle: @Hlnedemetriades

helene@helenedemetriades.co.uk

Hélène has been working as a transpersonal psychotherapist for 25 years. Her debut poetry collection 'The Plumb Line' was published in June 22 by Hedgehog Press. She is widely published in poetry magazines and anthologies and was the winner of The Silver Wyvern, judged by Robert Seatter, in the International Poetry On The Lake Competition, 2022.

Olivia D'Silva

See p. 263

https://oliviadsilva.com

YouTube & Instagram @resolutionpoems

My coaching practice is an integrated approach with co-meditation and poetry, that supports clients to welcome self-doubt, connect with their inner wisdom, and expand their capacity for life.

This is a deeply challenging but richly rewarding path.

Poetry is a healing creative expression of my belief in human resourcefulness and wholeness; that each of us is already enough, just as we are.

Julie Foubister

See p. 59, 157, 179

julie@thriverhive.comwww.thriverhive.com

www.thriverhive.com

Turning life's greatest challenges into opportunities for transformation.

Julie Foubister, Transformational Coach & Meaning & Purpose Practioner, Mindfulness & Meditation Teacher supports others in using the most challenging times as a catalyst for great transformation and peace of mind. Having personally experienced a Cancer diagnosis at the start of lockdown, Julie put together a programme to help others going through a similar journey.

Julie founded Thriver Hive to help people experiencing life changing events/illnesses to live a life they love now, rather than putting everything on hold in wait for better times, which Julie describes as the "I will be happy when…." Syndrome.

Gillian Gabriel

See p. 125, 167, 289, 291

gillian.gabriel@me.com

I am a Coach, Coaching Supervisor, coaching skills Facilitator, self-belief builder, gender equality warrior, wellbeing wonder woman, Poet and Writer. Through my business, The Stars Are Aligned Coaching, I empower others to live a life where their outer reality is aligned to their inner desires. I have 26 years' experience in management and leadership roles within the John Lewis Partnership with a large chunk of that time invested in Learning & Development strategy, design, delivery and evaluation. Personal growth has always been at the heart of who I am – I believe I am here to learn with, from and alongside others.

Elisabeth Goodman

See p. 215
tel 07876 130 817
www.riverrhee.com
www.linkedin.com/in/elisabethgoodman/

Elisabeth founded RiverRhee Consulting, specialising in "creating exceptional managers and teams" in 2009. She gradually brought coaching into her work, making it a core component after qualifying with Barefoot Coaching and the ICF in 2020-21.

Elisabeth enjoys helping individuals to exercise choice and realise their potential in the workplace by recognising their values and strengths. She is an advocate for neurodiversity, specialising in coaching for autism in the workplace and privately.

Experiencing the pandemic brought her closer to nature; she is now looking for ways to actively care for the environment, as well as bring it into her coaching.

Basia Henderson

See p. 159
connect@basiahenderson.com
https://www.instagram.com/basia.henderson/
or @basia.henderson

Basia Henderson is a Life & Leadership Coach and Remedial & Sports Therapist with a broad background and experience in education, business management, psychology and commercial real estate. In her free time she enjoys exploring psychology, mental wellbeing and spiritual teachings deriving from various ancient and contemporary traditions, with special love for Rumi and Dr Wayne Dyer. When inspired, she writes poetry around the topics of the spiritual nature of human experience and life, love and relationships, and healing. She is a fitness and wellness enthusiast and a forever student of life. Based in Scotland since 2005, born in Poland.

Julia Heubeck

See p. 31, 193, 213, 235, 295

Mob: +44 7814 485854

heubeck.julia@gmail.comwwww.juliaheubeck.com

www.juliaheubeck.com

Julia was raised in Germany until she moved to the UK for schooling and university. While pursuing a fulfilling career in Media, she hit a brick wall in her personal life and realized she needed to make some adjustments to her way of being. In 2018 she left her career and embarked on a journey of personal development, embracing a range of psycho-spiritual and somatic modalities. While she trained as a transformative coach, she is passionate about an integral approach, supporting other humans finding their North Star and a path through life that allows them to be their authentic self.

Frank Bolaji Irawo

See p. 187, 205

www.thecalmself.com

contact@letmebefrank.coach

www.linkedin.com/in/frankbolajiirawo

Frank Bolaji Irawo is an ICF certified Coach, Speaker, Poet. He works with Business leaders and entrepreneurs whose emotional well-being, wealth and relationships are suffering while growing their business or career. Helping remove mental blockers, unleash dormant creative energy, and rejuvenate business relationships to ignite productivity and fearless innovation. Getting the universe "flowing" in their favour resulting in the maximizing of their professional potential.

His book DREAM (ISBN: 1913905667); showcases his unique coaching approach using poetry as part of powerful transformative conversations.

He harnesses the power of words to awaken insight, and open doors of awareness that initiate transformation.

Leah Kaess
See p. 137
Leahkaess@gmail.com

Leah Kaess, JD, BCC, is a Board Certified Coach specializing in health and wellness. She helps her clients experience natural transformation through life's challenges, living increasingly in greater alignment with peace and happiness through a recognition of their true nature. Leah has coached executives for nonprofits and facilitated team-building and emotional intelligence retreats. Currently, Leah's coaching methods include Somatic Attachment Therapy, Internal Family Systems, Emotional Freedom Technique, and Positive Psychology Coaching. Previously, she was a public interest lawyer, representing abused and neglected children and people facing homelessness. She also taught at NYU School of Law.

Aidan Lazzarotto
See p. 49, 83, 177, 203, 255
coaching@aidanlazzarotto.com
linkedin.com/in/aidanlazzarotto/
www.instagram.com/transformativepoetry/

Aidan Lazzarotto is a poet, writer, speaker, storyteller, and transformative coach. Hailing from a rich family history of writers, teachers, and storytellers, his appreciation for the power of words began at an early age. His writing speaks to the innate beauty of our shared human experience, blending poetry, comedy, philosophy, and practical advice.

Aidan's coaching practice is an expression of his passion for mindfulness, stoicism, philosophy and personal development. His coaching integrates deep listening, transformative storytelling, and psychological principles to help clients discover a more beautiful experience of being alive.

Jennie Linthorst

See p. 73, 133, 223

Jennie.Linthorst@gmail.com

www.lifespeakspoetrytherapy.com

www.facebook.com/jennie.linthorst

Jennie Linthorst, MA, CAPF is the founder of LifeSPEAKS Poetry Therapy where she works with individuals exploring their personal histories through reading and writing poetry. She is on the faculty of UCLArts & Healing and presents workshops nationally including the East and West Coast Expressive Arts Summits. Jennie's poetry has appeared in *Bluestem Magazine*, *Edison Literary Review*, *Foliate Oak*, *Forge*, *Kaleidoscope*, *Literary Mama*, and more. Her poetry books are *Silver Girl* and *Autism Disrupted: A Mother's Journey of Hope*. Jennie has an M.A. in Spiritual Psychology, and certification in poetry therapy. Visit her website at *www.lifespeakspoetrytherapy.com*.

Lori Michael

See p. 47, 51, 225, 285

www.lorisstories.com

lorimichael@mac.com

Lori Michael has worked as a teacher, vocal coach, counselor, youth choir director, music director, and singer-songwriter. A songwriter since the age of eight, she established Lori's Stories (www.lorisstories.com) in 1993, bringing live performances of songs and stories to young children and writing custom songs. She also worked as a youth and family song leader in Boston area synagogues. While raising and homeschooling her son, she has continued to write songs, poems, and stories and is now in the process of recording and publishing them. Lori's prayer is that her poems and songs will uplift and inspire.

Debbie Moores

See p. 169

hello@debbiemoorestherapy.com

www.debbiemoorestherapy.com

I'm Mum to three grown-up and independent women, who I love and respect massively and are a huge inspiration to me. I have worked as an integrative/hypnotherapist since 2017, and enjoy combining hypnotherapy with other modalities, including art and writing as therapy. I feel honoured to be invited into individuals' private worlds in order to collaborate with them to access the parts of them that will allow them to live their lives by being more of who they are by releasing their limiting beliefs. I have always written to myself as a therapeutic release and for the purpose of processing my ideas and emotions.

Humaira Naz

See p. 15, 171

www.humairanaz.com

contact@humairanaz.com

Instagram: humairanaz.lifecoach

Hello, I am Humaira Naz, a Qualified Transformational Coach with a background as a Primary School Teacher, Special Educational Needs Coordinator, and Inclusion Leader. I also have studied Psychology and Sociology and am passionate about personal and professional development.

Supporting and empowering others to excel at their goals is key to the coaching work I do.

From a young age, I have found comfort by expressing myself through writing. As well as poems, I write articles for my blog, magazines and regularly journal. My wish is that others can gain joy and comfort by reading my work. Relax and enjoy.

Rama Krishna Rao

See p. 69

https://successklue.com

www.linkedin.com/in/connectwithramakrishnarao/

Rama Krishna helps individuals create businesses that work for them, not the other way around! He takes a unique approach that gives people the power to build businesses that support their lifestyles and dreams instead of forcing them to fit their lives into a business model. He says, "I have powerful conversations that change people's lives (one conversation at a time)" and further adds, "Build a business around who you are, not the other way around."

Susana Rinderle

See p. 65, 243, 257

wordswisdomwellness.com

purplelyrics.org

susana@wordswisdomwellness.com

Susana Rinderle, MA, PCC is a transformational life & leadership coach, trauma-informed resilience practitioner, and lifelong writer and poet. She won a poetry competition at age 17 and began performing spoken word in her 40s in New Mexico, where she placed fourth in two major slam competitions. A native of Los Angeles, her first career was in diversity, equity, inclusion (DEI) and leadership development, where she spent nearly 30 years garnering results for employers and clients across the U.S. and abroad in multiple sectors. Her articles and poems have appeared in multiple commercial publications, academic journals, and anthologies.

Todd Roache

See p. 109, 119, 271, 293

www.toddroache.com

todd@toddroache.com

I don't consider myself a poet, as much a person who uses words to survive this crazy thing called life. I only write poems when I'm slap bang in the middle of something intense, and those poems, those words are literally driftwood keeping me afloat and alive on the ocean of what I'm experiencing. Beyond that portrait, you could also say I'm a coach, a supervisor, an energy worker, a musician, a lover of nature, a lover of love, a lover of people, and an eternal student of mystery and magic.

Rona Rowe

See p. 85, 275

Rona@ronarowe.co.uk

+44 7808491604

I am a leadership coach, counsellor and writer. Born in Kuwait, educated in the UK and USA, I have worked in the arts, conference production, adult learning, public sector training and leadership development. Throughout my career, my roles have been about communication, connection and compassion – supporting individuals to create the lives and working worlds they want. My aim is to enrich the lives of those I meet and to experience each encounter as an opportunity to learn more about what is possible. Human beings amaze me. Writing poetry is one of the ways I make sense of the world.

Frances Simpson

See p. 75

francessimpson_@hotmail.com

I am a psychotherapist who has just completed four years of training in Relational Integrative Psychotherapy at SCPTI. I am also a mother of two children and a Psychology tutor at Coventry University, Scarborough. I started writing poetry early in my own therapy as a way to access feelings and to help attach emotions to events. I hope to start using this to help neurodivergent people to express themselves, as I myself have ADHD and my children are on the autistic spectrum and this is a subject close to my heart.

Alison Smith

See p. 95

www.thegardenway.co.uk

alison@thegardenway.co.uk

https://www.facebook.com/Thegarden111

Alison Smith is a Radical Alignment Coach and Creative Consultant for visionary, purpose led women. She is the founder of the Women's School of Metamorphosis, a training portal for women transforming the world through themselves.

Through creative practices, including poetry, she creates the conditions for each woman she works with to be seen – and so to see, know and love themselves, enabling them to live a creative life in alignment with their values and mission.

She divides her time between her physical home in Northumberland and her soul home in Crete.

Anna Springett
See p. 35, 103, 147, 217
anna@annaspringett.com

Anna Springett is a psychologist and coach of Irish-Finnish heritage. She works with leaders and teams, as well as supervising and developing coaching professionals. Anna is a gardener, artist and poet who loves trying new things, whether book genres or the food item on a menu that she has never heard of. She lives in Hampshire with a hairy husband, three beautiful daughters, and an emotionally needy Bernese Mountain Dog.

Richard Tyler
See p. 33, 37, 87
www.btfileadership.com
www.richardtyler.co.uk
www.willowtreefoundation.com

Coach, therapist, guide, author of Jolt!, storyteller, Isumutaq

Change is our only constant and as the world becomes more uncertain, conscious leaders are being required to step-up to navigate themselves and their people through new and unexplored terrains.

After a decade of playing lead roles in West End theatre productions such as The Phantom of the Opera and Les Miserables, Richard sees human potential through the artful lens of performance. Working this way enables him to hold the space for creative breakthroughs in which wisdom can reveal itself.

He works with organisations on every continent; CEOs, boards and senior leadership teams seek him out to coach, speak and facilitate workshops.

Janis Vogel

See p. 53, 135

www.janisvogel.com

www.instagram.com/janisvogel

Janis Vogel is a coach, writer and filmmaker. She draws on many modalities within her coaching practice: meditation, cognitive behavioral therapy, dance, reparenting. She guides her clients in walking through the world empowered to meet challenges and ready to embody healing and growth.

Janis is also a film editor. Her sensitivity and intuition create films which resonate joyfully, hilariously and heartbreakingly with viewers.

She is the co-founder of a 15,000+ member community, The Blue Collar Post Collective, a grassroots initiative revolutionizing the industry by proving that collaboration, rather than competition, leads to success.

Gillian Walter

See p. 29, 63, 163, 191, 249

gillian@inside-out-coaching.com

Gillian is a coach, supervisor, mentor, artist, owner of Inside-Out Coaching and author of a variety of poetry and artwork creative reflection books and resources including, Choir of Brave Voices: Creative Reflection for a Seasonal Journey of Self-Discovery. Accredited by the ICF, EMCC, EASC and CSA, her client work stems from creative, narrative and somatic coaching and supervision methodologies. British born, she now enjoys living and working in Switzerland with her family and Schnauzer.

Cara Wheatley-McGrain
219, 283
themindfulgut.co.uk
IG: mindfulgutuk
LinkedIn: Cara Wheatley Mcgrain

Cara is an educator, Hay House author, and accredited coach whose work integrates the core insights of self-compassion in holistic healing.

Cara is the founder of The Mindful Gut (UK) and works to support deeper insights into how our collective food choices shape both our outer and inner ecology. Her firm belief is that when we change our diet, we change the world.

Her work focuses on the themes of gut health, mental wellbeing and sustainability. She offers talks, workshops and retreats which embed somatic awareness, mindfulness and self-compassion to enable change.

Index of Poems by Themes

1. Connection

2. Love

3. Acceptance

4. Forgiveness

5. Resilience

6. Life

Milton Keynes UK
Ingram Content Group UK Ltd.
UKHW010308141124
451167UK00009B/290